THE LEGEND OF
ISTABRAQ

THE LEGEND OF
ISTABRAQ

Michael Clower

CASSELL&CO

To John Durkan

His life was cut tragically short, but
his memory will live on through the achievements
of one of the greatest hurdlers of all time.

Contents

1 Cheltenham Crisis

The bombshell struck shortly after 4.30 pm. Half-an-hour later alarm bells were ringing in television studios, newsrooms and bookmakers' shops. The horse expected to start the shortest-priced favourite in Champion Hurdle history was in trouble.

All had appeared to be going smoothly when Istabraq, who is notorious for becoming upset when his routine is changed, arrived at the Cheltenham racecourse stables at 4.00 pm on Monday, 13 March 2000. He had left Ballydoyle, just outside Cashel in County Tipperary at 8.30 am after doing his morning exercise, and had travelled in the stable's big blue horsebox to Shannon Airport, together with Theatreworld who is stabled in the next box to him in the yard reserved for the National Hunt horses at Ballydoyle. Theatreworld, second in each of the three previous runnings of the Smurfit Champion Hurdle, was again in the big race on the opening day of the famous festival. Darapour also travelled in the box to the airport. He was Istabraq's regular companion out at grass during the summer months, and he was due to run in the Ladbroke Casinos Final.

The three Aidan O'Brien-trained runners were outnumbered by the staff accompanying them. These included the stable's travelling head lad Pat Keating, Istabraq's lad Davy Clifford, Anita Harvey, who is in charge of the jumping yard, work rider Pat Lillis, farrier Ken McLoughlin and Tommy Murphy, the former highly successful jockey who is O'Brien's assistant. The flight from Shannon to Bristol went smoothly, and so did the journey from there to the racecourse in a horsebox organised by the shipping company. Clifford led Istabraq down the ramp and into the stable allocated to the horse. He took off the travelling rug and Anita carefully removed the protective bandaging from the horse's legs before putting on the padded wraps that Istabraq normally wears at home. She covered these with velcro bandages to stop the wraps slipping. Clifford brought out the hay that had also travelled from Ballydoyle, and looked on as Istabraq made himself at home in his new surroundings.

After twenty minutes the horse, as Clifford knew he would, began pawing at the sawdust. He got down awkwardly on to his knees and rolled over on to his back. He then struggled to his feet, shook himself and ambled over to the haynet in the corner of the box. Clifford looked at the bay with the large white star on his forehead, white socks and off-white hooves and felt as contented with life as the horse obviously was. For nearly three years Istabraq had been his principal charge. This was the third time he had been to Cheltenham with him, and Clifford was confident that the gelding would join the immortals by winning a third Champion Hurdle. Clifford turned away to get on with his other tasks, but Anita and the others kept half an eye on Istabraq.

It was Pat Keating who first noticed something was wrong. As he glanced over the door of the box, he thought the light must be playing tricks on his eyes. Just to be on the safe side and to satisfy his curiosity, he undid the door and walked quietly over to the horse. He had not been wrong. There was a trickle of blood coming down Istabraq's nostril. Keating was shocked. He looked closer. There was no dried blood; whatever had caused it had only recently happened. He called to Davy Clifford. The others inspected the horse in turn. It was Keating who made the decision – Aidan had to be told.

The travelling head lad always carries a mobile with him and he rang the office at Ballydoyle. O'Brien had stayed behind. The Flat season was about to begin and there were 130 of the best-bred and most expensive horses in the world to be got ready for it. The trainer wanted to supervise their morning work before travelling to Cheltenham by helicopter; he would fly back to Ireland immediately after Darapour's race. The girl on the switchboard put the call through, Keating explained how the horse had rolled and how he had noticed the trickle of blood. There was a stunned silence as O'Brien took in the implications. He asked to be told a second time what had happened and how the horse was. O'Brien said Keating should stay with Istabraq and he would ring him back.

O'Brien, thinking furiously, realised the blood could mean only two things – either Istabraq had banged his head when he rolled or he had some sort of haemorrhage. The first might not be serious, the second certainly was. The problem was finding out which. An endoscopic examination of the nostrils would answer the question, but in the past Istabraq had resented having a tube stuck up his nose to such an extent that he had to be sedated before he would consent to it. If the medicine used to sedate him was employed this time, traces of it would still be in his system the following day and he would eventually be disqualified amid a storm of recrimination. The trainer vividly remembered the scare when Istabraq had been found with blood on his nostril one day at Ballydoyle. It was after he had been moved from one box to another. O'Brien had called in the vet, had the horse scoped (under sedation) and he was found to be alright. Possibly the stress of the move had caused it. O'Brien had hoped it would prove to be a one-off. Seemingly it was not. If stress was again the reason, the omens were bleak.

At the racecourse the staff took it in turns to keep an eye on Istabraq. They had to be careful not to all crowd round the stable door, because they knew that would upset the horse and possibly make the bleeding worse. They debated what could have caused it. Like the trainer, they knew there were only two possible causes and they knew the implications. Istabraq would not be able to run if it was any form of stress-induced haemorrhage, and it might be too risky to let him take his chance even if it was just a bump. The bleeding could well be a symptom of something much more serious. It might even mean that the horse's racing career was over. Keating said he thought it must be a bump. He had often seen horses rub their heads against their knees when rolling and do it quite vigorously. Tommy Murphy had been with horses for nearly half a century and he had more experience than all the others put together. He looked closely at Istabraq's head and nose for any sign of a mark. There wasn't one and he feared a burst blood vessel.

Back at Ballydoyle, O'Brien had people to contact. One of the first was Charlie Swan who had ridden Istabraq in all his hurdle races and who was again expecting to be in the saddle the following day. Swan, also a trainer with a runner at Cheltenham, had taken a rare day off to play golf at Stratford in a competition that trainer Mouse Morris organises each year for the members of his appropriately named Birdie Syndicate. He was travelling back towards Cheltenham with Morris when his mobile rang.

'There is a bit of a problem with Istabraq, Charlie,' said the voice at the other end, and the jockey's heart sank. 'He rolled in his box in the racecourse stables and a bit of blood came out of his nose. I don't think there is anything to be alarmed about. We'll check on him in the morning.' But Swan *was* alarmed and so, he detected from the tone of O'Brien's voice, was the trainer. JP McManus, Istabraq's owner, was staying at the Lygon Arms, a fashionable hotel in the picturesque village of Broadway, some sixteen miles to the northeast of Cheltenham. He was a worried man when he heard what the trainer had to say and he feared the worst.

'I knew that there were a lot of people with Istabraq and if it had been just a case of the horse giving himself a bang, somebody would have seen it happen,' he reasoned. 'Either that or they would have been able to identify it. I didn't know what to think but when something like that happens, I tend to worry – and I did that evening.'

O'Brien's next port of call was the public. He consulted with Denis Hickey who, like Tommy Murphy, had a wealth of experience of such moments of crisis. Hickey had first joined the staff at Ballydoyle back in 1969 when the great Nijinsky was a two-year-old and two years later he had taken over as racing secretary. Apart from a short stint at Coolmore Stud, he had been at Ballydoyle ever since. O'Brien and Hickey composed a brief statement, saying that a trace of blood had been found on the horse's nostril after he had rolled and that a decision on whether or not he would run in the Champion Hurdle would be made in the morning. The statement was faxed to the Press Association. Within two minutes, it was on the newsdesks of pretty well every newspaper and television station on either side of the Irish Sea.

Keating's mobile rang. O'Brien, after asking how the horse was, said that the travelling head lad should let the racecourse know what had happened. The trainer did not put it into words, but Istabraq's bid to win a third Champion Hurdle was widely expected to be the highlight of the following day; if there was any possibility that the star might be missing, the stable had a duty to let the racecourse know. Keating went off in the direction of the office to look for the managing director. When he found Edward Gillespie, he rang O'Brien on his mobile and let the trainer pass on the bad news.

Most of the near 10,000 betting shops in Britain and Ireland were well inside the final hour of the day's trading when the news reached them. Many did not know what to do. The Champion Hurdle, with Istabraq expected to start at an even shorter price than Sir Ken when he won at 5–2 on for the second time in 1953, was a virtual non-event for the bookmakers. If he did not run, the race would be wide open and people would be much more likely to bet, but it would also be something of a anticlimax. Two of the most adventurous Irish firms, Paddy Power and Liam Cashman, had announced earlier in the day that Istabraq's third victory was such a formality that they were paying out all ante-post bets on the horse with immediate effect. It was an almost unprecedented move and a shrewd way of gaining publicity. Istabraq's setback though, left the advertising ploy with a hollow ring to it.

Aidan O'Brien, having fulfilled his obligations to the betting public with his statement to the Press Association, was concerned once more with the horse. He rang John Halley, the Ballydoyle vet, and asked him to accompany him in the helicopter the following morning. Halley, who of course knew that any examination would be restricted by the horse's refusal to be scoped, agreed to cancel his other plans and make the trip to Cheltenham. O'Brien found himself recalling what he had said to a visiting journalist twelve days earlier: 'This is Istabraq's fourth consecutive year going to Cheltenham and that takes some doing with any horse.' What he had in mind was that most racehorses have delicate constitutions, with their legs frequently unable to take the strain of their huge body weight, particularly when asked to exert themselves to the very limits of their capacity on either bottomless or firm ground. Few jumping horses stay sufficiently sound for them to make the same race-meeting four years in a row. That Istabraq's mishap had nothing to do with his limbs simply added to the bitter irony.

O'Brien rang McManus a second time and told him of his other calls. JP invariably wants his trainers to notify the press whenever any of his big-name horses suffers a setback so that there is no risk of punters being led astray. The trainer also rang Charlie Swan and said that the decision on whether to run would probably be based on whether or not Istabraq ate up his supper and his breakfast. If he cleared the pot, he was probably healthy. If he didn't, something was almost certainly wrong. The jockey was not reassured. He wondered if the air-conditioning in the plane had somehow caused a haemorrhage.

The Ballydoyle staff at Cheltenham had their supper at The Lodge, the hostel where most of them stay. It is regarded more like a hotel than a hostel, but Davy Clifford could not enjoy his meal. Nor could he sleep that night: 'I was very worried. I didn't know what had caused the blood to appear and I thought he probably wouldn't run.' Clifford and the others were up early. Even though Pat Lillis, Istabraq's regular rider, had travelled to Cheltenham, it had never been intended that the horse should be given a canter on the course like most of the other Irish runners. Istabraq is not ridden on the morning of the race on his visits to the meeting; he is just led out to stretch his legs. The same happened this time. Clifford knew how vital it was not to give Istabraq the impression that his routine was being changed in any way; he was worried that the horse would become stressed and bleed again. He was relieved to see Istabraq eat every bit of the scoop of nuts he was given for breakfast, but the uncertainty remained and the tension increased as the time for the trainer's arrival neared.

Charlie Swan felt much the same as Clifford, even though he had deliberately stayed away from the horse when he went to the racecourse stables that Tuesday morning to exercise No Discount, his runner in the following day's Royal & SunAlliance Novices Hurdle. The helicopter trip from Ballydoyle to Cheltenham racecourse takes ninety minutes, and O'Brien arrived with John Halley shortly after 10.30 am. For nearly three-quarters of an hour, O'Brien deliberated and consulted. Halley could find nothing wrong ('I thought he was OK but it was all a bit tricky'), and the situation was also discussed with McManus. At 11.30 am O'Brien shrugged his shoulders, swallowed and said quietly to those around him, 'It looks as if we run. Please God, we've made the right decision.' He promptly rang Swan and then informed the public via the *Racenews* reporter who was waiting at the entrance to the stable yard. But inwardly he was in turmoil:

> The horse seemed fine and there had been no further problems during the night. We still didn't know what had happened the previous afternoon, other than the blood appearing in his nostril. We didn't know either, where it had come from or what had caused it. We wouldn't know the answer until we'd scoped him and that was not possible. We could not examine the horse too closely either because he was on edge, very close to boiling point. He gets like that when he is near a race and we couldn't risk triggering him off. We would obviously continue to keep a close eye on him all the time up until the race. If it had been an ordinary race, we would not have run him, but what influenced us was that he was never going to get another chance to win a third successive Champion Hurdle. It was a big decision and a big risk. It put extra pressure on all of us and in many ways I felt we were doing the wrong thing by running him.

2 Worth a Fortune

Just before 4.00 pm on 23 May 1992 the cheering at the Curragh rose to fever pitch as Walter Swinburn and Marling got the better of a tremendous battle with Mick Kinane and Market Booster to win the Irish 1000 Guineas. At Derrinstown, some sixteen miles to the north-east, Cyril O'Hara looked at the mare for the umpteenth time that Saturday afternoon. She was in one of the two foaling boxes in what is called the private stud, to distinguish it from the public stud where the mares who are visiting the stud's own stallions are kept.

O'Hara, now the manager of the Ennel Lodge Stud near Mullingar, thought it ironic that the two best mares were the last to foal. Midway Lady, winner of the 1986 1000 Guineas and Oaks, had just done so. Now it was the turn of Betty's Secret. The mare turned uneasily in the large straw-lined box and seemed to be inspecting her swollen flanks. O'Hara was convinced she was only hours away. He was an old hand at the job but he could not help feeling a sense of excitement because this was going to be the best-bred foal of his year. It might even prove to be the Derby winner that is the ultimate achievement for everybody involved in Flat racing.

Four painful hours later, an exhausted Betty's Secret got to her feet and the foal she had just produced instinctively suckled her. The colt, who was to gain immortality as Istabraq, was a big bay, too big for the mare, and when Tom Deane arrived a few minutes afterwards he remarked to O'Hara: 'If Betty's Secret has any more foals, she'll be lucky. This one has knocked a lot out of her.' The stud groom's words were to be proved prophetically correct but Deane, like O'Hara, had races like the Derby in the forefront of his mind for the newborn foal.

Not for one moment did he imagine that the gangly colt would become one of the most famous hurdlers in history.

There was no reason why he should. The colt was by Sadler's Wells, one of the best Flat racing stallions of all time. A son of the equally influential Northern Dancer, Sadler's Wells had been trained by Vincent O'Brien to win the 1984 Irish 2000 Guineas, Coral-Eclipse Stakes and Phoenix Champion Stakes; he was also second in that year's French Derby and in the King George VI and Queen Elizabeth Diamond Stakes. He has been an even bigger success as a stallion, repeatedly being champion sire in Europe where he has been responsible for more Group winners than any other stallion. His success has been reflected in his covering fee which is now 150,000 Irish guineas. As he has sometimes produced more than 100 foals a year, he has proved to be a veritable gold-mine for the Coolmore Stud, which has also enjoyed spectacular success with several of his sons.

The pedigree of the new arrival was just as good on his mother's side. Betty's Secret was bred to produce top Flat racehorses like her own sire Secretariat, one of the few horses to win the American Triple Crown. She never raced but her half-brother, Caracolero, won the French Derby and her grandam produced Majestic Prince who won the first two legs of the 1969 Triple Crown, as well as producing the 1971 Dewhurst winner Crowned Prince.

Betty's Secret was owned by Eddie Taylor, the legendary Canadian breeder who stood Northern Dancer and bred Nijinsky. Northern Dancer was the obvious choice for Betty's Secret's first mate, not least because Taylor had ready access to the stallion. The few nominations that came on the market were priced at $800,000. As a general rule, a mare's first foal tends to be less successful than the later ones but Betty's Secret struck gold immediately. At least she did on the racecourse. Taylor was disappointed that he received only $340,000 for the offspring at the top Keeneland yearling sale. The colt was bought by Luigi Miglietti as a prospective stallion for his stud in Venezuela, named Secreto and sent to David O'Brien at Ballydoyle.

The young O'Brien used his father's gallops but had his own yard on the opposite side of the main training area to that of his father and sent his horses out early in the morning before the parental eye was up and about. The pair would often meet for lunch at the house of Vincent O'Brien, but David seldom discussed either his horses or his training methods with his father. Instead he kept everything to himself, worried incessantly and worked longer and longer hours in his pursuit of perfection. He was a brilliant trainer, who almost certainly would have been as good as either of the other two O'Briens who made Ballydoyle their own. But he could find no answer to the self-imposed ever-increasing pressure and in 1988 he stunned the racing world when he announced that he could not carry on. He was only thirty-two and had been training for less than eight years. He eventually turned his talents to producing wine. He would, surely, have rewritten racing's record books if he had stayed with the family business.

He had his greatest moment at Epsom in June 1984 when Secreto got the better of the supposedly unbeatable El Gran Senor to win the Derby by a short head after being driven along all the way up the straight by Christy Roche. Pat Eddery, in contrast, had been so confident of victory that he had sat motionless until well inside the final furlong when he found to his horror that the tank was empty. Vincent O'Brien, who trained El Gran Senor, was proud of his son's achievement in becoming at twenty-seven the youngest man to train the winner of the Derby, but he was mortified that it had come at the expense of a colt he considered one of the best he had ever trained.

A half share in Secreto was sold for $20 million and the value of Betty's Secret also soared. She visited Northern Dancer three more times, but of the offspring, two were fillies who never raced and the colt, Classic Secret, won only once. He was bought by Vincent O'Brien for $1,400,000 as a yearling. He was retired to stand at Tony O'Callaghan's Tally-Ho Stud outside Mullingar, but in 1994 he was sold to the Azienda Agricola Loreto Luciani Velletri near Rome. When Istabraq started to win Champion Hurdles, O'Callaghan tried to buy him back but the stallion's Italian owners said the horse was not for sale.

Betty's Secret was a prolific breeder, a trait she inherited from her dam who produced eleven foals and her grandam who had twelve. Betty's Secret produced one every season for twelve years but in comparison with her first, none of the others were all that good. Four of the six fillies never ran, but the yearlings that came on the market regularly earned Taylor a million dollars or more. In 1987 he sent the mare to Ireland to visit the best of Northern Dancer's sons in the British Isles, in particular Sadler's Wells. He boarded her at the Ballysheehan Stud owned by Philip Myerscough and his wife Jane, a daughter of Vincent O'Brien.

Two years later Taylor died in the Bahamas and Betty's Secret was bought by Hamdan Al Maktoum, the second eldest of the four fabulously wealthy Maktoum brothers of Dubai, in a private deal believed to be worth $6,000,000. She was in foal to Sadler's Wells but the colt, named Mutamanni, failed to win when trained by Dick Hern in England or when sent to race in Dubai. At the 1995 Tattersalls July sales he was bought by Tony Mullins for a mere 3000 guineas before being sold on to Mark Roper. The Curragh trainer tried schooling him over hurdles but surprisingly, considering how good a jumper his full brother was to become, Mutamanni showed no aptitude at all. He aggravated an old tendon injury and was sold to Turkey as a stallion.

Sheikh Hamdan owns the 850-acre Shadwell Stud in Norfolk, but it was to Derrinstown that he sent Betty's Secret. The County Kildare stud comprises 2000 acres but it was much smaller when Hubie de Burgh bought it in 1983 – it was a condition of de Burgh's appointment as Sheikh Hamdan's Irish stud manager that he should find a suitable stud. It belonged to Anne, Duchess of Westminster and was where Arkle spent his final years.

Tom Deane, a tall man with a fondness for wearing a peaked base-ball-style cap, is the son of a County Kerry farmer. He was not born when Arkle was racing and he was only twenty-two when he first went to Derrinstown in September 1989, after working at the Airlie Stud in Ireland, Grangewilliam in New Zealand and the Circle O Farm in Kentucky. He quickly learned to treat Betty's Secret with respect:

> She was a fusspot but also a real tough lady, and she could be
> a bit difficult to handle. The mares always pal up in groups of
> two or three when they are out in the paddocks and most of
> them, once they're in their group, settle quite happily and won't
> attempt to fight each other. Betty's Secret was different. If she
> ever got her buddy in a corner, she would whip round and lash
> out at the poor mare.

Betty's Secret was twice sent to Mujtahid after producing Istabraq. It was in many ways a surprise choice of stallion after Northern Dancer and Sadler's Wells. The 1990 Gimcrack winner had no Northern Dancer blood in his pedigree and he was not particularly successful as a stallion, but Sheikh Hamdan felt that the family needed an injection of speed. She went into foal in successive years but probably because of the exertions she suffered producing Istabraq, she was unable to hold the pregnancy. It was decided to retire her and when she later developed a sinus problem, she had to have an operation. Eventually it was colic that claimed her and she died eleven days before her son won his second Champion Hurdle. At Deane's suggestion, she was buried beneath a triangular patch of grass at the top end of the stud.

The stud groom remembers each of his charges like a benevolent schoolmaster recalling his prize pupils, and he took photographs of Istabraq and the others as they grew up:

> Istabraq was always easy to handle, he never showed any signs
> of temperament and he was a very correct individual from day
> one. Foals will normally turn their feet out a bit or show signs

of weakness in their joints in their early days, but Istabraq was unusually correct. When they were galloping round the paddocks, he never looked any faster or better than the others, but what was different about him was the way he showed himself off. It was almost as if he knew he was worth a fortune.

Deane believes in mixing with the foals and twice a day he would walk through the paddocks, keeping a wary eye out for any cuts and bruises, and at the same time encouraging them to make friends with him. Within weeks of birth, even the shyest will walk up to him to have its nose fondled and its neck patted. Istabraq was less than a fortnight old when he began trying to get some of his mother's feed out of the trough and learning to push his way in among the other foals as they all helped themselves to the mares' evening mash – oats, bran and Gowla breeder (protein, vitamins, calcium, salt, phosphorus, etc) mixed together with hot water.

As the autumn weaning time neared, Deane put the feed into white tubs in the paddocks, ostensibly for the mares, but also to give the foals an element of familiarity for the time when their mothers would no longer be there. As the youngest foal on the stud, Istabraq was in the last batch to be weaned. Betty's Secret was taken to the top end of Derrinstown, as far out of earshot as possible and Istabraq was put with seven of his regular companions into a paddock. Once Deane was satisfied that the eight foals had become used to being without their mothers and that they were eating happily out of the white tubs – the morning feed was oats and nuts in a mix – they were transferred to Windgates, two or three miles away.

This part of Derrinstown is near the Barberstown Castle hotel and is now used as an isolation unit in the event of coughing or disease. In 1992 it was the base for all the weanlings, and Gus Roche, the Windgates stud groom, took over responsibility for Istabraq. The son of a blacksmith in Doneraile, the County Cork village whose church steeple was the finishing point for the first recorded steeplechase back in 1752, Roche had ideas of becoming a jockey. He joined local trainer John Joe Walsh when he left school and rode in point-to-points for two seasons before turning his back on life in a racing stable to work at Gay O'Callaghan's Yeomanstown Stud on the outskirts of Naas. He switched to Derrinstown in 1986 and was thirty when Istabraq joined him.

Istabraq was turned out into the paddocks during the day, still in the same group of eight, and brought in at night, but once the warmer weather arrived in the late spring he was left out all the time. From early August, he spent much more of each day in a stable. He was also walked

Aidan O'Brien had
people to contact.
He notified Charlie
Swan, JP McManus and
the Press Association in
quick succession.

It was Pat Keating who
first noticed something
was wrong. The stable's
travelling head lad was
shocked.

Tommy Murphy.
He looked closely
at Istabraq's head
and nose for any
sign of a mark.
He feared the worst.

Tom Deane....
'There are two things you don't bet against - one is United, the other is Istabraq.'

Sadler's Wells...
150,000 Irish guineas a time....The famous stallion gallops round the paddocks at the Coolmore Stud.

Mutamanni, Istabraq's full brother, 'who showed no aptitude at all'- with his disappointed Curragh trainer Mark Roper.

Three weeks old. Istabraq with his dam, Betty's Secret, in the paddock at Derrinstown.

Gus Roche.... 'There was never anything to suggest he was going to be special.'

Sheikh Hamdan bin Rashid Al Maktoum, over 300 horses in training, and a fondness for Arabic names.

Five months old. The day before he was weaned, with his mother in the background.

'He was just another ride.' Istabraq goes down to the start for his first race at Doncaster in November 1994, ridden by the stylish Gary Hind.

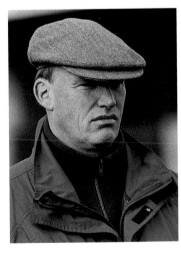

John Gosden, a commanding figure with Derby ambitions.

The first time he reached the frame. Istabraq
(Tony McGlone) is beaten a length and a half by
Silktail (Gary Carter) in the Jif Lemon Handicap
at Newmarket.

Willie Carson, five
times champion,
seventeen British
classic wins and fourth
in the all-time British
list.

'I couldn't believe it.' Despite all Willie Carson's efforts, Istabraq is beaten by a neck by En Vacances (Timmy Sprake) at Newbury in October 1995.

Aged eleven, John Durkan prepares to ride out with the family's string.

John Durkan with his
mother, Beatrice, on the
eve of his wedding.

At Stanley House. JD
and stable jockey
Frankie Dettori smile for
the camera.

Riding Crammer over the Grand National fences at
Aintree. JD was also third on this horse in the
Foxhunters at Cheltenham.

with a groom leading him and once he had become accustomed to this, he was lunged. Roche remembers Istabraq well, even though he noticed nothing exceptional about him apart from his pedigree:

> He was a placid yearling, good natured and relaxed. But there was never anything to suggest he was going to be special – or not special for that matter. He was basically an average yearling. Naturally, I followed his progress but I was disappointed to see that he needed a mile and six by the end of his three-year-old career. With his pedigree, I'd hoped that he would have been better, perhaps even the real thing. The one time I went to watch him race was when he won at Punchestown in April 1997. I remember noticing that he had not grown that much, and nor was there much change in him physically. It is only since then that he seems to have filled out.

Roche has never backed Istabraq: 'the price has always been too short', but he has watched all his Cheltenham wins in the stud's tea-room which is invariably packed during the week of the festival.

'It's a great atmosphere in there,' says Deane, who each year gives the benefit of his advice to the other workers in the stud. 'The lads are always trying to pick out something at a good price, and invariably some of them suggest a horse to beat Istabraq. I always say "Listen, there are two things you don't bet against – one is United, the other is Istabraq. They're both champions".'

Hamdan bin Rashid Al Maktoum, minister for finance in Dubai, has over 300 horses in training and he believes in giving them all Arabic names. These frequently sound mysterious and confusing to the European ear and their translation into English can also cause difficulties because there are old Arabic meanings as well as current ones. Istabraq means silk in modern Arabic, but Sheikh Hamdan said that the translation he had in mind when he named the horse was lightning or lightning-fast. Unfortunately, so far as his breeder was concerned, Istabraq failed to live up to the expectations conjured by his name.

The Sheikh has more than twenty trainers in England, Ireland, America and Dubai. He alone decides who should train which horse, although John Gosden made a point of going to see the yearlings at Windgates in the autumn of 1993, partly out of interest and partly because he felt he would have a better chance of getting the ones he wanted if he was able to make his preferences known.

John Harry Martin Gosden, 6 feet 4 inches and long since partly bald, cuts a commanding figure on the racecourse and he is a

THE LEGEND OF ISTABRAQ

particularly eloquent speaker. His father, Jack 'Towser' Gosden, trained Aggressor to win the 1960 King George VI and Queen Elizabeth Stakes, and would have trained Charlottown to win the Derby six years later had not ill-health – severe heart problems – forced him to give up training at Lewes in Sussex at the end of the horse's two-year-old career.

Jack Gosden was sixty-two when he died in October 1967 after suffering a heart attack. His only son was a sixteen-year-old pupil at Eastbourne College and only just beginning to come to terms with the fact that his rapidly growing frame had destroyed his hopes of becoming a jockey. His father had advised him against a career as a trainer, pointing out that he would be on call twenty-four hours a day, seven days a week. Instead he went to Emmanuel College, Cambridge to study land economics and then to Venezuela to work in land development. But horses were in his blood and he would often go to the local racetracks in the early hours of the morning to watch the horses work under floodlights.

He had been in Venezuela for less than a year when he wrote to Noel (later Sir Noel) Murless to ask him for a job. The Newmarket trainer was one of the most successful of all time, and after working as his assistant for two years, Gosden moved to Ireland to continue his racing education with Vincent O'Brien. He was also O'Brien's assistant, but he realised he would have better prospects in California when he flew out there with several of the Ballydoyle horses that were to be sold at Hollywood Park. After learning the ropes with the ex-Irish Tommy Doyle, he set up on his own in October 1979 with just three horses. Success, thanks partly to the support of Robert Sangster, came quickly and he made his name with the Eclipse Award winners Bates Motel and Royal Heroine, who won the Breeders' Cup Mile in the Sangster colours in 1984.

He was widely recognised as one of the leading trainers in North America by the time Sheikh Hamdan and his brothers decided he was the man they wanted to be their principal trainer in Newmarket. There was almost two years between the initial approach and Gosden agreeing to return to Britain at the end of 1988. The historic Stanley House stables on the Bury Road was soon housing more than 150 superbly bred horses, and expectations were high that the new trainer would make an immediate impact.

John Gosden sent out seventy-seven winners in his second year and eighty-four in his third, but the best of the Maktoum horses were with Henry Cecil at Warren Place and Andre Fabre in Chantilly. The ones at Stanley House tended to be backward and nowhere near as good. Gosden, who was later to admit that he was not particularly happy in his first few years at Newmarket, found himself the subject of some vicious back-biting amongst racing's sharp-tongued gossips who were claiming that the new man was not doing as well as he should. Neither Keen Hunter's victory in the 1991 Prix de l'Abbaye nor Wolfhound's success in the 1993 Haydock Sprint Cup (also a Group One race), failed to silence the critics who were unwilling to recognise the type and quality of horses Gosden had been given. Unfortunately, it soon became clear to the trainer that Istabraq, despite his illustrious pedigree, was yet another of the many slow-maturing horses he had somehow to get the best out of. Gosden decided he would have to adopt a patient policy with the colt:

> I took a lot of interest in him, but he was backward and it was pretty obvious that he wouldn't want to be asked any questions early. He showed some potential as a two-year-old, but it was clear that his first season was not going to be the time for him. Instead it would be the time for him to develop. He did a little bit of work towards the end of that season. It was satisfactory, but no more than that and he didn't strike me as a classic horse. His first race was not until Doncaster at the beginning of November and at that stage I just wanted to get a run into him.

The race was a seven furlong maiden and Istabraq opened up second favourite of the nineteen runners – the bookmakers had a much healthier regard for Gosden's ability than the gossips and this was a particularly well-bred colt. It was only when they discovered that there was no money for the horse, that the layers allowed him to drift out to 8–1. The ride went to Gary Hind, a Newmarket-based jockey who had partnered thirty-one winners that year and who had ridden for Gosden since 1989. He had also ridden Istabraq at home.

'John is usually pretty laid back with his orders. It was more or less a case of go out there and look after him,' Hind recalled. 'At the time Istabraq was just another ride for me but he ran well.'

Istabraq showed his inexperience by losing ground at the start, but he improved steadily throughout the last two furlongs to finish eighth. He was beaten less than five lengths by the winner, and while there was nothing to indicate that the race was anything other than a pretty ordinary maiden, the way he kept on at the end suggested that Istabraq had a future. However, Sheikh Hamdan and his advisers already thought that it was not going to be the sort of future suggested by the colt's exalted pedigree. 'If a horse has a lot of ability, no matter how backward he might be, you will always know about it when he is still a two-year-old,' said Angus Gold, the Sheikh's racing manager. 'There was never any talk of that with Istabraq and so we realised by the end of 1994 that he was not going to be anything special.' Indeed Istabraq's limitations were confirmed on the Newmarket gallops early the following year, as Gosden recalled:

> He had improved, but we hadn't given him any fancy entries because he seemed to be a solid galloper as opposed to one with gears and a turn of foot. He would go well enough in his work but when the other horses he was with turned the heat on in the last two furlongs, he stayed in the same gait and in the same rhythm.

Istabraq's Pedigree

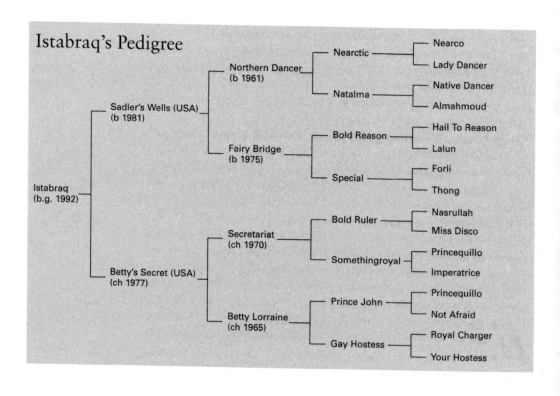

3 He Couldn't Quicken

Willie Carson, retained as first jockey by Sheikh Hamdan, had the mount when Istabraq reappeared in a ten furlong maiden at Kempton at the end of April 1995. Carson, then fifty-two, had been champion five times and was nearing the end of a distinguished career that was to see him with seventeen British classics and take fourth place (behind Sir Gordon Richards, Lester Piggott and Pat Eddery) in the all-time British winners' list. Carson, a Scotsman known for his cackling laugh, later joined the BBC's racing team. He had a deceptively busy style of riding, often pushing his mounts before any of the other jockeys but invariably having a bit more up his sleeve than his rivals. He frequently appeared to snatch races out of the fire and he was popular with the punters who admired his refusal to give in, particularly on those occasions when their money seemed lost. He could also be outspoken, even blunt.

'I put Istabraq into the race at Kempton, but he couldn't do it and so I left him alone,' he recalled. Istabraq weakened over three furlongs from home and finished halfway down the field. The promise he had shown at Doncaster had all but evaporated, and the colt fared no better when tried over a similar trip at Chester just under a fortnight later. Carson was scrubbing along by halfway and his mount finished with only three behind him: 'he had no experience, and he had no pace,' was how the jockey summed up the performance.

Even worse, the horse was found to have problems with his near fore soon after his return to Newmarket. The vets were called in and x-rays revealed a small piece of chipped bone in front of the fetlock joint. This is the joint which the cannon-bone makes with the pastern and it roughly equates with the ankle of a human being. The normal practice would be for the horse to have an operation to remove the piece of bone, but after much deliberation, it was decided to leave it where it was. This 'floating chip' is still there today.

The problems with the joint kept Istabraq off the racecourse until the end of July. In the interim the Derby was run on a Saturday for the first time since 1953, and had it not been for the once-raced Lammtarra who was making his seasonal début, Gosden would have had both first and second. He saddled Presenting and Tamure, who looked like winning when he led inside the final furlong only to be caught close home. Every Flat race trainer's ambition is to win the Derby, but Gosden had particular reason for wishing to do so after his father had been so cruelly robbed of his great chance. Tamure's narrow defeat was an equally bitter blow.

Istabraq finally returned to the racecourse on the last Saturday in July. Carson was at Goodwood for the Nassau Stakes and the Stewards Cup, and the ride on the Sadler's Wells colt in the Jif Lemon Handicap went to Tony McGlone. The then thirty-two-year-old is a useful light-weight, if a little unfashionable – his twenty-eight winners that year put him only forty-fourth in the table. The race was Istabraq's first in handicap company and it was confined to horses rated no higher than seventy. In other words the class was moderate, much more so than the maidens he had been contesting, and Istabraq had top weight of 9st 7lb. The distance was a mile and a half, almost two furlongs more than the race at Chester and Istabraq started second favourite. The pace was slow and McGlone found he was able to match strides with the leader. With just over half a mile to run, McGlone kicked but his hopes of victory were dashed when Gary Carter cruised up on the favourite Silktail approaching the furlong marker. For the first time in his life, Istabraq found himself in a battle. He didn't flinch and while he was unable to peg back Silktail, he refused to give in and he made the favourite work for it all the way to the line.

Willie Carson scented victory when he rode him at Salisbury in a maiden race just under three weeks later. The distance was a mile and three-quarters, which was clearly in the horse's favour, and the fact that Carson had bypassed the final day of York's big August meeting to ride at the comparatively humble Wiltshire course was not lost on the punters. Istabraq started at 6–5 on:

> He ran very green, I don't know why but he did and he
> struggled to win. I tried to ride a race on him and I nearly got
> him beat as a result. He seemed to need a lot of time to do
> things. I was riding him from three furlongs out and

approaching the furlong marker, I thought he was beaten but from then on he outstayed the others. I felt he wanted even further and that he had to make the running. I decided that in future I would send him to the front and let him use his stride. But I thought he would always be vulnerable because he couldn't quicken.

Gosden decided to strike again while the iron was still hot and thirteen days later Istabraq was sent to York for the Batleys Cash & Carry Handicap over a distance just short of a mile and three-quarters and worth £8090 to the winner. This was a 0–90 handicap and Istabraq had been raised 6lb since the Jif Lemon. He was only fourth favourite with Frankie Dettori's mount Celeric being the one punters wanted. This gelding by Mtoto was conceding 13lb to Istabraq, but he was a smart stayer who was to win the Ascot Gold Cup two years later.

After a furlong Carson decided to send Istabraq to the front but when the tap was turned on at the two furlong pole, the colt was headed although it was only by a head that Celeric beat him. 'It was very tight at the finish, to-and-fro, and Istabraq was not giving in,' recalled Carson. 'My fellow again gave me the impression that he would get further and Celeric, as we now know, was a very decent animal.'

Istabraq next went to Ayr for the Bogside Cup, a 0–75 handicap, over an extra furlong. He was rated 75 – he had gone up another pound after York – and he had top weight of 9st 7lb. There were twenty runners but the form book said Istabraq and he started 6–4 favourite. Carson elected to go to Lingfield where he had several fancied mounts and John Gosden booked Pat Eddery for Istabraq. Eddery, then forty-three, had been champion ten times and he immediately took to the colt:

We made all the running. The ground, although officially good, was a little on the slow side but Istabraq travelled easily all the way. He kept on well in the final two furlongs to beat Boundary Express (ridden by Istabraq's original partner, Gary Hind) by two and a half lengths. In the end he won quite comfortably. He didn't feel slow in any way but I thought he would stay two miles and I also thought that he would be a better horse with another year over his head. I could see him developing into a decent Flat horse.

Gosden was pleased. 'Pat got him into a lovely rhythm out in front, really using his stride and this race was when Istabraq showed me precisely what he was capable of, as well as the way he wanted to be ridden, i.e. making all the running.' Gosden decided to aim the colt at the Tote Cesarewitch Handicap on 14 October and Istabraq was made favourite.

Three weeks before this rich two and a quarter mile race, Istabraq was sent to Ascot for the Gordon Carter Handicap over two miles. It was the last race on an extremely valuable card that featured the Queen Elizabeth II Stakes, and Carson won the big race with an inspired ride that has earned a place in racing folklore. The going was good but this had been one of the hottest and driest summers in Britain since records began, and the Ascot course had been repeatedly watered to stop it becoming firm. However, in the back straight much of the ground nearest the far rail had been protected from the sprinklers by over-hanging trees. Carson found that it was firm and therefore much faster. While Bahri's pacemaker, Muhab, set off in front on the inside rail and was followed by the opposition, Carson headed for the trees, losing several lengths as he steered a course round the wide outside. It was an audacious move that would have had the press writing him off as overdue for retirement if it had not come off. However, the plan worked because Bahri had a clear lead as the field approached the final turn where Carson steered back towards the inner to come home six lengths clear of the brilliant Irish filly Ridgewood Pearl, with the rest well strung out – most notably Muhab who trailed in a long way last, his decoy tactics having played a major part in the sensational victory.

Carson hoped to follow up in the Gordon Carter. Istabraq started favourite but he was being ridden along at halfway, and five furlongs from home he was last of all. He finished only eleventh of the sixteen runners and Gosden's worst fears were realised when he got the horse home to Newmarket.

'He had been hurt in the same joint that had given trouble after Chester, the one with the floating chip in it,' said Gosden. 'I'm sure it happened as he was going down the back straight. It scuppered our plans for him, including the Cesarewitch.'

Istabraq was able to return at Newbury five days after the famous Newmarket handicap, but the two mile Vodafone Group Handicap was only a 0–90 affair worth just a fraction of the Cesarewitch. Istabraq had 8st 10lb, he started second favourite and Carson was confident of victory. 'The ground was starting to turn – it was good to soft. We led, and I kicked early because he stayed so well and because I knew he would keep going,' Carson said. 'But we were beaten a neck by En Vacances ridden by Timmy Sprake and trained by George Foster. I couldn't believe it. I'd heard that they fancied En Vacances a bit, but I still didn't expect him to beat us.'

En Vacances, who was receiving 12lb, went on to finish second in the following season's Cesarewitch so it was a better performance than it looked at the time. Istabraq ran only once more that year, when he was disappointing in a two mile handicap at Doncaster. Carson, who blamed the good to firm ground, never rode Istabraq again but he frequently goes to the Cheltenham festival and he has followed the horse's career with considerable interest:

> On the Flat I put him down as a slow maturing type and a slow
> learner. He also lacked speed and was not at home on fast
> ground. He needed plenty of time to do things. I don't think he
> ever sweated up much before his races with me and he was
> rather a cold type of horse in that he didn't show much
> character or emotion, he just got on with it. On occasion
> I suspected his honesty. He always made hard work of things
> and I sometimes thought he was a bit of a lad who might have
> needed a pair of blinkers. But I came to the conclusion that the
> reason he was struggling was because he had no speed. In fact,
> he was one-paced. He probably still is.

That final observation is a little surprising, given how Istabraq can demolish his opponents with a devastating burst of speed over hurdles. Carson has watched this, considered it carefully and left his opinions unchanged:

> National Hunt horses are not as good as those on the Flat
> where everything happens that much quicker, particularly on
> firm ground. It's also a matter of adapting and maturing. A lot
> of horses improve if they are given the time and I can
> remember Dick Hern having a very similar animal called
> Persian War. He wasn't that good on the Flat but he trained
> on and won three Champion Hurdles.

The year 1996 began badly for Istabraq and his trainer. Several of John Gosden's horses were found to be suffering from muscle enzyme problems, and as a result, the stable had few winners in the early part of the season. In addition some of his best prospects suffered setbacks; while Istabraq was not considered to be among the stable stars, he had developed problems with his feet, particularly the front ones, and they were causing repeated headaches for Gosden:

> He was flat-footed and we had a lot of trouble keeping the
> heels sufficiently elevated off the ground. We often had to put
> bar shoes on him to do this. He always wore bandages at home
> and early in the season he developed a quarter crack. This was

a split in the hoof wall running upwards. It had to be patched,
and for three weeks he was confined to walking and trotting.

Gosden's own problems became public property at the beginning of
June when *The Sporting Life* carried a feature article entitled 'How Good
is Gosden?' It was a highly critical assessment of the trainer's record and
compared it unfavourably with that of Andre Fabre, who also trained for
some of the Maktoum brothers. It is rare for trainers to be subjected
to this sort of newspaper criticism. Football and cricket
managers, particularly those of the English national teams, have to
endure merciless persecution in the press, but trainers who have a not
dissimilar job, are rarely criticised – not because racing journalists are a
more benevolent bunch than soccer writers, or because their editors are
any less demanding. They are not, but the relaying of information about
trainers' plans for their key horses forms an important ingredient of
their copy – and those who bite the hand that feeds them inevitably
go hungry so far as this sort of news story is concerned. The Gosden
article, because it was so unusual, created far more waves than it would
have done in other sports, and the man on the receiving end was to admit
years later that it had hurt him badly. The gossips, needless to say, had a
field day.

David Ashforth, who wrote the article, likes to portray himself as
the bumbling college lecturer he once was but he is one of the most
talented in his field. When *The Sporting Life* closed in 1998, he was one
of the few of that paper's writers to be given an automatic transfer to
the *Racing Post*. His boldness in penning the Gosden article brought him
criticism from some but the admiration of his fellow writers who voted
him the racing journalist of the year.

A week after the article appeared, Istabraq finally made it back to
the racecourse. As Willie Carson was riding the fancied Alhaarth in the
Derby – Gosden was again out of luck, with Shantou finishing only
third – the mount in the Penny Lane Handicap at Haydock went to
Richard Hills who was the owner's second jockey.

Istabraq, according to Gosden, was not fully wound up. Apart from
the problems with the horse's feet, the trainer had not been able to get as
much work into him as he would have liked because it had been a
particularly dry spring and the ground was too firm for Istabraq to be
risked on it. As usual, Istabraq made the running but when he was
headed by Turgenev approaching the furlong marker, he could not
quicken and was beaten a length. Sheikh Hamdan decided he had
persevered long enough and he gave Gosden instructions that he did not
want to keep four-year-olds unless they could be guaranteed to win
Group races. Istabraq was entered for the following month's Tattersalls

July Sales. His subsequent success over hurdles has reminded Gosden of his time in California and of his thoughts in his early days at Newmarket:

> When I came back from America in 1988, I would pick up the *Horses In Training* book and see trainers who had eighty two-year-olds, seventy-five three-year-olds and about six older horses. I used to think to myself what happens to all these horses? Why do we not have a racing programme for them? Why are we finishing the careers of horses before they have even got all their teeth at the age of four? I found it shocking. The sadness of Flat racing is that so many horses go wrong because too much is asked of them too soon in life when they are not mature enough to take it, or they are sold abroad and are lost to the racegoing public. So few horses are able to come through the system. I wouldn't mind if they became no more than great old handicappers. At least people would get to know them. Unfortunately our racing system and the tradition that goes with it, doesn't allow that – and I think it is a great error. The one thing I am proud of with Istabraq is that we gave him every chance to develop. He had to have a lot of care as a young horse and, if he hadn't been given that, he would never have made it. If we had pushed him and forced him, we would have ruined him for life. The list of horses who could have gone on to become something special, but got destroyed at two and three, is very long. I love to see a horse get better and better each year and become a family name, like John Henry in America, Desert Orchid in England and now Istabraq. These horses mean a lot because they become part of folklore and this is what racing should be all about.

Less than a year after Istabraq left him, Gosden answered his critics once and for all and ended his family's run of misfortune in the Derby, when Benny The Dip won the race that meant so much to him. Less than three seasons after that, he said goodbye to Stanley House to move to Manton to train once more for Robert Sangster. By that time, tragically, the first person to recognise Istabraq's real talents was dead.

John Durkan was born in the City of London Hospital on 23 February 1966. He was the fourth eldest and the second son of the nine children of Bill and Beatrice Durkan. The Durkans believe in large families and when Bill boasts that he has 500 cousins, he is only partly joking. He has seven brothers and most of them are in the building trade from which they have all made their fortunes, after starting life in humble circumstances in a thatched cottage in Bohola in County Mayo.

By the time John was born, his father had expanded his one-man plastering operation into a thriving business and was living in Tufnell Park in north London. After the Durkans had two more children, the family returned to Ireland to live on the outskirts of Dublin at Stepaside, not far from Leopardstown racecourse. John went to the national school in Kilternan and then to Benildus College in Kilmacud. By this time his father, now an extremely wealthy man, had bought a large piece of land halfway up a hill with commanding views over Stepaside and the rest of Dublin. He built, not just a house, but a racing stable as well. He shed four stone to ride in point-to-points before striking gold with a mare called Anaglogs Daughter who he trained to win the 1980 Arkle Trophy by twenty lengths.

John was fourteen and already hooked on racing. When Anaglogs Daughter won the Buchanan Whisky Gold Cup at Ascot later that year, he accompanied his father to the Royal Box to meet the Queen Mother. So did several of his uncles, plus their families and friends. There were so many Irish people trying to get into the box that they had to take it in turns.

John progressed from his father's stables to spending his summer holidays at the nearby Flat racing yard of Seamus McGrath. When he left school, he did a course at the Irish National Stud and in 1989 he left Ireland to take a job with Charlie Brooks, a well-known jumping trainer in Lambourn, with his father's blessing only reluctantly given. Bill Durkan thought he should join elder brother Danny in the family business. He knew from his own experience that racing was a tough game and privately he wondered if John was strong enough to take all the knocks he felt were sure to come his way. He also knew that there was a lot more money to be made from building houses.

In addition to learning the ropes with Brooks – John planned to become a trainer eventually – he was also riding as an amateur. This meant that he did not get paid when he rode in races and he shared a house at Ashdown near Lambourn with Eddie Hales, Ed Dunlop and Jamie Osborne. Henry Daly was also there for a time. All are now trainers, but they led such a noisy, riotous existence outside working hours that they were known as the Brat Pack. 'It was a very lively house,' Hales remembers, 'JD was the quietest of us. He was the best mate in the world and all the birds fancied him. Many of them came to see him, and so the rest of us benefited.'

After two and a half years with Brooks, Durkan joined Oliver Sherwood – who also trained jumpers in Lambourn – to work as his assistant while continuing to ride in races. He twice took part in the

Grand National and he was placed in the top amateur races at Cheltenham – the National Hunt Chase, the Foxhunters and the Kim Muir. He rode nearly 100 winners and was one of the few to have ridden winners for both the Queen and the Queen Mother. When he rode for the latter, he shook hands and said: 'I've met you before, Ma'am.' The Queen Mother looked at him and searched her memory, but without success. 'When was that?' she asked. He replied that it was when Anaglogs Daughter won at Ascot. The grand old lady of jump racing might sometimes forget a face, but never a horse. She immediately recalled the occasion, looked at the young man in front of her and said: 'Ah yes, you have a large family.'

Bill Durkan, having long since accepted that his racing-mad son was not going to join the business, hoped that he would return to Ireland to take over the stables above Stepaside. But John had made his name in racing in England and he was convinced that his best chance of success was there. He also decided that he should train mainly on the Flat, rather than concentrate on jumpers. There is more money in Flat racing, the owners are wealthier and the horses are sold on to be replaced with new ones every two years, whereas jump trainers have to walk a frequently nervous tightrope to keep their horses – many with bad legs after years of wear and tear – in one piece.

Durkan sought out some of the top Flat trainers to see if they would give him a job, so that he could learn about how they train their horses. He also spoke several times to Anthony Stroud who was Sheikh Mohammed Al Maktoum's racing manager and therefore in an extremely influential position. It was suggested that John Gosden might fit the bill, particularly as Durkan had ridden a winner for him, and in June 1994 he moved to Newmarket to become assistant trainer at Stanley House. Two months later he got married.

4 Drama at the Sales

Carol Hyde was twenty when she first met John Durkan in August 1989. With long blonde hair, the slim and attractive Carol was the sort who would catch any young man's eye. Practical and sensible, often serious, she was the perfect foil for Durkan's wilder side. She is one of five children of Timmy and Trish Hyde who live at Camas Park, a large house surrounded by a considerable acreage of first-class stud land in County Tipperary, just off the road between Cashel and Dundrum.

Tim Hyde, Timmy's father, trained at Camas Park after finishing a highly successful career as a jump jockey. He rode Workman to win the 1939 Grand National, and he won the 1946 Cheltenham Gold Cup on Prince Regent before finishing third on the same horse in that year's Grand National. He also won the 1942 Irish National on Prince Regent as well as the 1938 race on Clare County. He combined race-riding with showjumping, but at the 1951 Clonakilty show the horse he was riding fell and rolled on top of him. He was so badly hurt that he spent the rest of his life in a wheelchair.

Timmy assisted his father and also rode as a professional jump jockey. He did not enjoy the same big race success but he did win the Cathcart at the 1969 Cheltenham festival on Kinloch Brae, on whom he also won the following year's PZ Mower Chase at Thurles. It was when he retired from the saddle, though, that he found his *métier* – spotting the potential in young horses and selling them on. He buys foals and yearlings and sometimes three- and four-year-old unbroken store horses, before taking them back to Camas Park to develop and eventually be resold, invariably at a profit. He has been so successful at selecting foals and selling them as yearlings that he is known as the 'king of the pinhookers'. One of his most notable and most profitable triumphs came with Authaal, the 1986 Irish St Leger winner. He bought the son of the ill-fated Shergar for 325,000 guineas as a foal and sold him at Goffs less than a year later for Ir3,100,000 guineas, a European record that was to stand for fourteen years until Hyde sold a Nureyev colt at Newmarket for 3,000,000 guineas. He had bought that one as a foal for just $360,000.

His only son Tim, who is a practising vet, rides as an amateur, and the four daughters all have connections with racing. Valerie, who rode winners, is also a vet and she is married to John Osborne, another vet and successful pinhooker. Wendy is the wife of Eddie O'Leary, a blood-stock agent and dealer, while Janet, the youngest, works for Simon Sherwood and is the long-time girlfriend of Norman Williamson.

Carol is the middle one of the five, and when she was fourteen she informed her father that she too wanted to ride in races. For what seemed to his daughter like several minutes, Timmy Hyde considered the suggestion. 'Well, we'll think about it,' he said eventually. 'But don't you ever ask to ride over hurdles or fences.'

It was not until several years later that he allowed her to start riding in bumpers and she won on her fourth ride, Oak Melody, at Dundalk in May 1989. Not long afterwards, her father relented sufficiently to permit her to ride in point-to-points. She won two races in Ireland and later four in England. She has also won eleven races on the level. In addition she was a successful three-day event rider and for a time was a member of the Irish team. Shortly after meeting John Durkan, she moved to England to work for Henrietta Knight at West Lockinge as a pupil-cum-assistant. She had no real ambition to become a trainer, but she loved the life and was keen to learn. The job also enabled her to continue race-riding. West Lockinge is no more than ten miles from Lambourn, and she and Durkan met again and began going out together. They were married on 19 August 1994 and the reception was held at Camas Park.

They went back to Newmarket where Carol rode out for Michael Stoute and her husband studied how a top Flat race trainer operated. He was still riding in races whenever he got the chance, but he never rode the racehorses at Stanley House because they were young and he was considered too heavy for them. To begin with, they lived in Newmarket at the Egerton Stud before finding a house at Cheveley, a couple of miles outside the town. During the winter, when Stanley House had no runners, they would fly back to Ireland for the weekend and go racing.

Early in 1996, Durkan decided that he would start training later that year. He discussed the matter with his father on one of those trips home, and explained why he felt he should train in England rather than attempt to expand the family's small training operation in Ireland. Bill Durkan understood and generously offered to foot the bill for the purchase of a training stable. Many trainers struggle to make the business pay because they are crippled by big rents or repayments on large loans. Durkan would be saddled with no such burden and therefore would have a much better chance of surviving the first few crucial seasons.

He told John Gosden that he would be leaving him in the autumn when the yearling sale season started. Gosden already knew that Durkan was only going to be with him a comparatively short time. It is accepted that most assistant trainers are there to learn the job and their relatively low salaries take this into account. There was therefore no ill-feeling on the trainer's part. Durkan's next task was to find people prepared to put horses with him. He made a point of telling many of the owners he knew that he was taking out a licence towards the end of the season. His wife said much the same to her own wide circle, some of whom were based in Ireland. Several of those the pair approached promised to send them a horse or two, others chose to ignore the hint. Durkan knew that many of the promises would fail to materialise, but even allowing for that, he reckoned he had enough to see him start off with forty horses.

He was also searching for suitable premises and when he heard that Tom Jones was retiring, he went to see him. Jones trained at Newmarket at Green Lodge and his principal owner was Sheikh Hamdan. Jones was seventy-one and had been training for forty-five years. He had made his name with jumpers like Frenchman's Cove and Tingle Creek, but he also trained several classic winners. Green Lodge was beyond the reach of most aspiring young trainers but Durkan's father was a wealthy man and a sale was agreed. Durkan and his wife had a brochure printed to give to prospective owners, with the new master of Green Lodge posing at the front gate of the stables. The brochure also contained photographs of Durkan winning in the colours of both the Queen and Sheikh Mohammed and of Carol riding a winner for John Gosden.

When he heard from Gosden that Istabraq was to go to the sales, Durkan mentally ran through the list of those who said they would send a horse to him. He had never ridden Istabraq, but even though he knew all about the problems with the horse's feet, he had a high opinion of him and was convinced the horse would make a top hurdler. The gulf between a staying Flat handicapper and a good hurdle race horse is often bridged, but many more fail to make the transition. However, Durkan was convinced that Istabraq would do so and rather more surprisingly, he believed that this was a horse who could win at Cheltenham. 'He is no soft Flat horse. He is the sort who does not get going until he is in a battle,' he told one prospective owner. 'He has more guts than class and that's what you need. He will win next year's SunAlliance Hurdle.'

Racehorse trainers tend to make such bold predictions. Most have enormous faith in the horses they train and in their own ability to win

Camas Park, the Hyde
family home.

Right; JD on Her Majesty The Queen's Carpathian at
Windsor in August 1995.

Below; JD with two other members of the Brat Pack, Eddie Hales (left) and Jamie Osborne who was his best man.

Above; Wedding day, August 19 1994.

Below; Fagan (left) and Machine share in early married life at the Egerton Stud at Newmarket.

Opposite; Carol is led in after winning on the John Gosden-trained Mukeed at Newmarket in August 1996. Her husband is immediately behind the horse.

Carol on Top Of The Mark at Boekelo in Holland.
That evening JD rang to tell her he was feeling ill.

Another brochure
photograph.
JD with one of the
horses at Green
Lodge.

Aidan O'Brien....The call
of racing became all-
consuming.

Istabraq strides out on his way to the start of his
first hurdle race at Punchestown in November 1996.

The mistake that cost him the race. Charlie Swan
sits tight but Noble Thyne (Tommy Treacy) is able to
regain the initiative.

First victory over hurdles. Istabraq easily accounts for the opposition in the Avonmore Royal Bond Novice Hurdle at Fairyhouse in December 1996.

Istabraq looks into the camera in the Fairyhouse winner's enclosure.

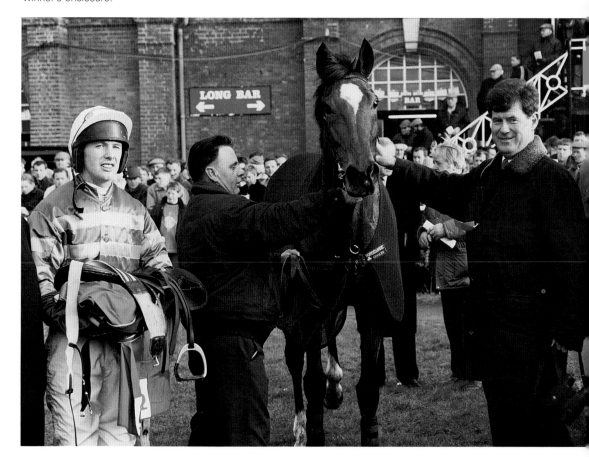

Controversy at Leopardstown. Istabraq is far from
fluent at the last in the Deloitte and Touche in
February 1997. Finnegan's Hollow (Conor O'Dwyer)
jumps it much better.

Only a head to spare.
The finish of the
Deloitte and Touche.

John Patrick McManus,
hooked on gambling
from an early age.

Istabraq's feet have
tested him to the
limit....Ken McLoughlin
at work at Ballydoyle.
Note the tools of his
trade on the left.

Below; Safely over the last in the Royal & Sun
Alliance Novices Hurdle. On the far side is amateur
Fred Hutsby on Mighty Moss, and Daraydan
(Richard Hughes) is jumping the final flight.

Posing for the cameras. Travelling head lad Pat Keating is to the right of the horse's head and far right is Tommy Murphy, no stranger to the Cheltenham winner's enclosure.

Opposite; Returning in triumph.

The girl from County Donegal. Anita Harvey, who is in charge of the jumpers at Ballydoyle

Davy Clifford....
Ambitions now centred
on being associated
with the best.

Finnegan's Hollow falls heavily at the last at Tipperary in October 1997. He lay winded for ten minutes but he was lucky not to break his neck.

Istabraq sweeps over the last to win the first
running of the John James McManus Memorial
Hurdle by seven lengths.

The rain is still
coming down. Bridie
McManus (centre)
twice lent her son
money to keep him
in the bookmaking
business.

Charlie Swan reports to JP and Aidan O'Brien. Also
taking a keen interest is Michael Tabor who has a
major share in most of the Flat horses at Ballydoyle.

Ed Byrne, the photographer who provided some of
the pictures for the brochure, visited John Durkan
during his last few days at his parents' home.

1998 AIG Europe Champion Hurdle. Istabraq is clear
of His Song (Richard Hughes). Noble Thyne
(Graham Bradley), who beat Istabraq in his first
hurdle race, is just about to jump the hurdle.

JP listens to Swan's
report in the AIG
winner's enclosure.

A sombre moment. Carol receives the AIG trophy from Taoiseach Bertie Ahern. Her father, Timmy, is on the far left.

A tribute to John Durkan. Carol poses with Istabraq on the day after her husband's funeral.

good races with them. Owners, who also tend to look on those who carry their colours as swans rather than geese, like to hear this sort of fighting talk. The pessimistic trainer, and there are few, needs to have extraordinary ability and achieve tremendous results if he is to attract owners. Needless to say, most such predictions tend to be replaced by excuses for why the horses were beaten and by further ambitious plans.

The more Durkan thought about Istabraq, the more determined he was to buy him. He thought he had an owner for the horse but a week or two before the sale, when Durkan tried to get the man to commit himself, he backed out. Durkan searched desperately for someone to take his place. One of those he had spoken to and who had offered to give him a horse was JP McManus. The legendary Irish gambler had known Durkan's father-in-law for a long time and even though he had little interest in Flat racing, he admired the way Hyde's skill in selecting foals had repeatedly paid off. However the problem, as Durkan was only too well aware, was that McManus preferred buying horses that looked exceptional when winning a bumper or a maiden hurdle than those off the Flat, who already had a lot of mileage on the clock. Durkan spoke to Timmy Hyde once more and again impressed on him his belief in the horse. Hyde said that he would buy him if Durkan could find nobody else. But it was not the sort of shrug-of-the-shoulder promise a rich man might make to please his son-in-law and more particularly his daughter. This was a horse and Hyde was a horseman. He was not going to dispense with basic principles. He therefore went to Stanley House to examine Istabraq and to talk to the man who trained him.

Shortly after he had satisfied himself he was not buying trouble, Hyde bumped into McManus. He went back to Durkan and asked him to write down the relevant details about Istabraq, so that he had a piece of paper to show JP. Durkan tore a page out of a sales catalogue and scribbled out this brief summary:

ISTABRAQ. Won 2 of his seven starts last season. 1 mile 6 fur maiden at Salisbury on good-firm ground. Was second in next three starts before winning competitive 2 mile h/cap at Ayr, soft ground. Favoririte [sic] for Cesarawitch. Went over the top and did'nt run.
Feet: Flat footed and wears bar shoes if and when feet give trouble. $1/4$ crack in first week of April. Walking and trotting for 3 weeks. Back in strong work after that rest and feet have been no problem since. Ran at Haydock 3 weeks ago. Finished 2nd giving the winner $2^1/2$ stone.
Apart from feet which are no major problem, he has a floating chip in OF joint which he has had since a yearling

and gives him no trouble at all. Touch wood he has always
been a very sound horse who in my opinion goes on any
ground except firm.

Durkan's spelling and punctuation may not have been his strongest
points, and nor on this occasion was accuracy. 'Giving the winner $2^1/_2$
stone' represented an exaggeration of 40 per cent. Interestingly, he wrote
that the floating chip was in the off-fore whereas Gosden is convinced
that it was in the near fore.

The Tattersalls July Sales took place over three days and coincided
with the Newmarket July meeting, with selling starting at 9.30 am each
morning, breaking off before lunch and resuming at 5.45 pm, half an
hour after the last race. The ten horses from Stanley House were sold on
the first evening; two were owned by Sheikh Mohammed and five by
Sheikh Hamdan. None of the ten wase that special, indeed one had been
hobdayed, another had been seen to crib-bite and wind-suck and only
two of them had won a race.

McManus did not go to the sale, and neither had he set much store
by John Durkan's hand-written note, nor by the Cheltenham-winning
prediction that had been passed on to him by Timmy Hyde:

I'd heard that sort of thing said so many times before, and it's
only the odd time that it actually works out. But I'd said to
John that I would be more than happy to have a horse with him
and he was very bullish about this one, so I had said I would
buy him. However, I like to have some sort of plan made before
a sale, otherwise it's a case of another bid, then another. We
didn't know exactly what he was going to make, although
Timmy thought it could be 100,000 guineas, possibly a bit
more. I left the exact limit to him, but I said we ought not to
pay much more than that.

Durkan went to the sale with his wife and her father and it was agreed
that Hyde should do the bidding. John and Carol were nervous. They
had convinced themselves that Istabraq would make six figures and
might well go for more than the rather vague limit set by McManus. It
was a relief when the bidding proved to be much weaker than they
thought and the hammer came down at 38,000 guineas. It was the
highest price of the first day and only one horse in the whole sale made
more. McManus, though, was delighted when Hyde rang to tell him
how little the horse had cost him.

John and Carol, going through the sale again afterwards, suspected
that Istabraq's foot problems were the reason that there was not more

interest in him. Carol had noticed that the pasterns were down when the horse was being led round the ring and she suspected half of Newmarket knew that he always wore bandages at exercise. This would suggest that Istabraq had problems with his legs, a much more serious matter than poor feet. However, Angus Gold thought the price reasonable:

> All our horses come to the point where we decide either to send them abroad or to sell them and as Istabraq stayed too far to race in Dubai, we felt that this was the right time to pass him on. He certainly wasn't without ability, but he was short of Group class. Every one of our horses goes to the sales without reserve and they make what the market thinks they are worth. I felt it was a relatively good sale and I don't think anybody should allow their minds to be clouded by what Istabraq has done since. It has to be said that at the time of the sale, he was a one-paced galloper who had problems with his feet and who did not have a turn of foot. While he was a tough horse who would act on easy ground, I would have questioned whether he had enough speed to be a good hurdler.

The day after the sale, arrangements were made to ship Istabraq to Ireland. The negotiations to buy Green Lodge were at an early stage – Tom Jones intended to continue training there until the end of the season in early November – and renting stables there would have involved unnecessary expense. It was decided that the horse should go to Camas Park until he could be brought back to Newmarket later in the year.

Soon after Istabraq's arrival in County Tipperary, Hyde rang John Halley and asked him to geld the horse. Removing the testicles is standard practice for a horse being sent jumping. Those left as entires tend to think too much about the opposite sex and if they brush a hurdle or a fence with such a delicate part of their anatomy, they understandably become reluctant participants. They are also easier to handle if they are gelded. Halley lives near Fethard, some fifteen miles from Camas Park, and is widely considered to be one of the best in the business. Gelding is a straightforward operation, but quite frequently the older the horse is the longer it takes him to get over it. Istabraq was badly affected. He lost condition and it took a lot out of him. He was turned out into the paddocks and it was not until well into September that it was felt he had fully recovered. Towards the end of the month he began to resume a normal training routine, just walking to begin with, then walking and trotting. The delay in the return to training did not bother McManus. 'There was no great urgency with him,' he said. 'At that stage Istabraq was just another horse.'

John Durkan was still at Newmarket working for John Gosden and making plans for filling the boxes at Green Lodge. He had orders to buy yearlings for several owners and he was working hard on persuading others who were slightly less committed to follow suit. The biggest yearling sale was the Houghton in the first three days of October. As it was in Newmarket, it was easy for Durkan to attend but the sky-high prices were out of his range and his frame of mind was not helped by having a bad cold. At the end of the three days he felt terrible, almost as if he had flu, but he was sure he had no temperature.

Carol was in Holland with the Irish three-day event team; when he rang her on the evening of the final day of the sale and told her how awful he was feeling, she urged her husband to see their doctor. Convinced he could be suffering from nothing worse than a cold, he ignored his wife's advice. The following Tuesday the big Irish yearling sale at Goffs was due to start and he knew he would have a better chance of buying horses there because the prices would not be so high. He flew to Dublin to spend the weekend at his parents' home.

Beatrice Durkan took one look at her son and told him he must see a doctor. This time he did as he was told and on the Saturday he was prescribed a course of antibiotics. He was, he told his mother on his return to the house, 'dying of the cold'. She was concerned, but no more than any mother would be in the circumstances and she suggested he go to bed. On Monday morning he was no better and Beatrice Durkan rang her own doctor. She took her son to the surgery and the doctor prescribed more antibiotics, but this time much stronger ones. Durkan, despite feeling even worse, went to the sales on Tuesday and again the following day. When he returned on the Wednesday evening, he looked dreadfully ill and his mother came to the conclusion that he had pneumonia. She insisted that he should give the final day of the sale a miss. The following morning it was all he could do to get out of bed. Beatrice Durkan rang the doctor again, and was told to take him to St Vincent's Hospital for tests. X-rays were done on his chest and blood-tests were taken. He went home to bed. By this stage, he accepted that it was pneumonia. Carol, contacted in Holland, decided to abandon the rest of the three-day event and fly to Dublin. John's mother was starting to worry.

'He was perspiring a lot and we were repeatedly having to change the sheets,' she said. 'It was obvious that he was really ill, but I had never known anybody with pneumonia before and I assumed the sweating was normal. Then we got the results of the tests. The blood-count was terribly low, and when I heard that I immediately thought he must have leukaemia. I still don't know why I thought that. I didn't know anything about the disease, but that was what went through my mind.'

The doctor who rang from St Vincent's Hospital that fateful

Thursday afternoon said that he should return to be admitted for treatment and further tests. By this time he was hardly able to walk and he said little as his mother accompanied him back to the hospital. That evening Beatrice Durkan was told that her premonition was correct. Two days later John began a course of chemotherapy.

Leukaemia is a cancerous condition in which the number of white corpuscles in the blood is permanently increased. It is characterised by changes in the marrow in the bones and by the enlargement of the lymph glands all over the body. Although there are a number of recognised treatments, there is no specific cure, and many who suffer from the disease are eventually killed by it. It was a harrowing prospect for a man of only thirty, about to embark on a career for which he had been planning for a third of his life. It was just as bad for his wife and his parents. Beatrice Durkan tearfully remarked to her husband that while she expected her parents to die before she did, it was hard to accept that one of their own children was going to go first.

There were a number of pressing decisions to be made. Carol, sitting beside John in his hospital bed, talked to him about what they should do about Green Lodge. The contracts were due to be signed the following week. The doctors in St Vincent's had stressed that the treatment would last for quite some time and that recovery would take even longer. Carol and her husband decided that their plans to take over the Newmarket stable should be put on hold. Bill Durkan spoke to Tom Jones; he was impressed when the veteran trainer expressed sympathy and understanding to such an extent that he was prepared to scrap the deal. He also said that if John recovered he would still sell him the stables. The racing press were then told of John's decision and the reason for it.

Bill Durkan wondered whether his son should continue treatment in Ireland or go to America. His mind was made up when he met John Halley. The vet told him that his own wife Susie had had cancer and had gone to Florida for treatment and made a full recovery. Durkan made further inquiries and he discovered that the hospital with the best reputation for treating leukaemia was the Sloan Kettering in New York.

At the same time as the racing press were notified, Carol and John contacted the owners of the horses he had bought. Most made arrangements to send their horses to other trainers, but there was more involved with Istabraq. He was under the care of Carol's father and he was the one above all others that John wanted to train if he should recover. Timmy Hyde and John discussed the matter with McManus. John pointed out that Aidan O'Brien was highly successful, he already trained for JP and that there was no better training establishment in the world than Ballydoyle. McManus agreed, subject to the proviso that Istabraq would join Durkan 'once he got better and started training'.

5 Flat-footed

Aidan O'Brien is the third eldest of the six children of Denis O'Brien, a County Wexford farmer who was a particularly successful point-to-point rider. He won 140 races, mostly on horses trained by himself. He also rode a few bumper and hurdle winners, but he was too heavy to consider a career in racing. His primary occupation was, and still is, the farm at Killegney near Clonroche which has been in his family for generations. His wife Stella also comes from a farming background and the tradition has been carried on by their son, Walter. There are two other brothers in addition to Aidan – Denis works in the transport business and Tom is a mechanic. Denise is a nurse while the other sister, Elizabeth, is married to Shay Slevin who trains near Enniscorthy. She is also involved with the training and this had long been Aidan's ambition. When he left school, his father entrusted him with his six point-to-pointers but everything went wrong and none of them even made the racecourse. Denis O'Brien fixed him up with a summer job picking strawberries and then a more permanent one in the mill at Clonroche. He was employed by the Waterford Co-op and began at the bottom, sweeping the floors before moving to driving a fork-lift truck.

After eight months the call of racing became all-consuming and he left to work for PJ Finn (a brother-in-law of Charlie Swan). Two months later Finn decided to leave his Curragh base and O'Brien moved to Jim Bolger high up in the hills on the Carlow/Kilkenny border. He was only seventeen and he relished the hard-working environment. He also began to make his name as an amateur rider. He stayed with Bolger for three and a half years, leaving in August 1991 to join his future wife, Anne Marie Crowley, who had taken over her father's stable at Owning near

Piltown that year. Anne Marie was expanding her training operation rapidly and at the end of the 1992/93 season, when she became Ireland's first woman champion jumps trainer, she handed over the licence to her husband. In his first season Aidan was champion trainer with a record amount of prize money and was also champion amateur.

He developed an uncanny knack of being able to run his horses often without them losing their form. Part of his secret was a supremely testing gallop, built up the side of the hill immediately behind the stables. This enabled the horses to be made fitter with less galloping than on a conventional, more level gallop. When the great Vincent O'Brien (no relation) decided in October 1994 to retire, his son-in-law John Magnier invited Aidan to take over the training centre at Ballydoyle. O'Brien was a few days short of his twenty-fifth birthday and had held a licence for less than eighteen months. However, Magnier, who had built up the Coolmore operation into the most successful stallion stud in the world, is a great believer in youth. He is also a shrewd judge and he was convinced he had spotted a genius. He backed up his judgement by offering to put a string of superbly bred horses with the young O'Brien.

He was a little surprised when O'Brien said he would accept the offer provided he continued with all the jumpers at Owning, twenty-five miles away. For over three seasons he ran both stables and at one stage he was champion trainer on the Flat and over jumps. He is a modest, almost shy man who goes to inordinate lengths to make his horses happy in their work. It is his instinctive understanding of a racehorse's mind that has had a lot to do with his phenomenal success. He was quite happy to train Istabraq until such time as Durkan was able to take him over:

> I knew John from riding against him and I'd always found him
> to be a proper gentleman. I remember Istabraq arriving at
> Ballydoyle – he went there rather than Piltown because JP's
> other horses were at Ballydoyle. He was only rated eighty-
> something on the Flat, but John obviously saw plenty in him
> because he told me when the horse was still with Timmy, that
> he would win the SunAlliance Hurdle. That was a very tall
> order for a horse who had never even run over hurdles. John
> also told me that he was a bit of a fretter.

Istabraq had been jumped over poles at Camas Park to teach him the rudiments of his new career and Carol rode him a few times. The next step was to school him over hurdles, but there were none at Ballydoyle in October 1996, so he was taken to the Curragh seventy miles away. Charlie Swan was stable jockey for the O'Brien jumpers and he drove up from his home in Cloughjordan that morning:

We jumped him over the baby hurdles a couple of times and then we put him over five of the eight hurdles on the schooling ground. I couldn't believe how good a jumper he was. He was quite amazing, a real natural. Not once did he try to duck out or run away from a hurdle. I think I'm the only person ever to have jumped a hurdle on Istabraq and that trip to the Curragh was the only time we took him away from Ballydoyle to school. Soon after that, Aidan put up a row of six baby hurdles alongside the main gallop and six bigger ones on the other side of it. We schooled him over these and he was every bit as good as he had been that morning on the Curragh.

John Durkan's treatment at the Sloan Kettering Hospital was already underway when Istabraq made his jumping début. The hospital is in Manhattan and friends lent Carol an apartment in Central Park West so that she could be near her husband. Later, when his condition worsened, she would often spend nights in the hospital. Beatrice Durkan also took up residence in New York. The secretary at Camas Park faxed John extracts from the *Racing Post* and other papers whenever she thought there was anything that would interest him. One item was the report of Istabraq's run in the two mile Locks Restaurant Novice Hurdle at Punchestown on 16 November.

Istabraq started second favourite that Saturday but odds-on was Noble Thyne, who was trained by Paddy Mullins and who had form credentials infinitely more impressive than those of Istabraq. He had won three bumpers, and he had only been beaten a head in the Deloitte and Touche Novice Hurdle, a recognised Cheltenham trial, at Leopardstown the previous February. The conditions of the race were all against the six four-year-olds because Noble Thyne, despite being two years older and having won those bumpers, had to give away only 5lb.

Those who backed Istabraq from 7–4 to 6–4 were unaware that Swan went into the race almost with his whip hand tied behind his back. McManus does not approve of his horses being given a crack with the stick in their first race over hurdles in case they associate jumping with pain. He was not at Punchestown that Saturday and he had not given any direct instructions to Swan, but the jockey was only too well aware of the owner's views. Aidan O'Brien also wanted to ensure that Istabraq enjoyed the experience. Swan was to drop him out and if the horse proved good enough, produce him going towards the last.

It was only at that point that things did not go according to plan. Istabraq was travelling the better when he narrowly headed Noble Thyne at the final flight, but he promptly made a mistake, lost the initiative and was beaten a head. Significantly, the third, the useful Saving Bond, was twenty lengths back. That evening Swan rang McManus, as he always does when the owner has not been at the races. He refrained from saying that if he had been allowed to use his whip, he would have won. Instead, he diplomatically said that he had been as kind to the horse as he could and that he thought Istabraq was the sort to do well over hurdles. What he did not put into words was his impression that the horse would probably need two and a half miles, if not three.

Swan, then twenty-eight, had been champion in each of the previous seven seasons, and he had already ridden more winners in Ireland than any Irish-based jump jockey has ever done. He was born in Ireland, but he is the son of British parents. He is descended on his mother's side from Tom Chaloner who rode Macaroni to win the 1863 Derby. His father was a captain in the First Queen's Dragoon Guards while his maternal grandfather was an officer in the Indian Army. Swan's father also rode as an amateur and he took part in the 1975 Grand National. Swan, who served his apprenticeship with Kevin Prendergast at the same time as Kieren Fallon, worked his way up the racing ladder the hard way to become an outstanding jump jockey despite a succession of injuries, most notably to his arms. Rarely for a top sportsman, he keeps his deep-seated determination to win hidden within a modest, considerate and understanding personality. No request has ever been too much trouble for him, no matter whether it's a small child wanting an autograph, a journalist looking for a quote or a trainer wanting him to get up before dawn to school a horse.

During the fortnight after the Punchestown race, Aidan O'Brien could detect evidence of improvement in Istabraq, both in his work and in his well-being. He knew that the horse had been nothing like fully wound up for his first run, and he expected him to turn the tables on Noble Thyne in the Avonmore Royal Bond Novice Hurdle at Fairyhouse fifteen days later. In addition to the Punchestown winner, there were three others in the £25,000 Grade One race who had won their most recent starts, including the English raider Lake Kariba. This time Istabraq started favourite and there was no necessity to adopt patient waiting tactics. Swan had him in the first two throughout and sent him away after the third last to beat Palette with ease. Noble Thyne was beaten almost twenty lengths. O'Brien was delighted:

> To say we thought Istabraq was going to be something special
> at that early stage would be rather a big statement to make, but
> I felt he could prove to be really good when he ran in a race
> where there was a strong pace throughout. Charlie had a lot of
> faith in him. The horse had so far done everything we asked of
> him and he had done it well. He had been bought by John with

the SunAlliance Hurdle in mind, but he was showing us that he had loads of pace, certainly enough to consider the two mile Supreme Novices Hurdle as an alternative to the SunAlliance which was over another five furlongs.

The one slight cloud on the horizon was Istabraq's foot problems. O'Brien believes these are not helped by the hooves having so much white in them. This, he maintains, makes them softer than the normal black hooves and more prone to cracks. The person who became most involved with them was the Ballydoyle farrier, Ken McLoughlin. Then thirty-two, McLoughlin came from Dublin and his family have been farriers for seven generations. His grandfather had five forges in different parts of Dublin in the days when horses were commonplace in the Irish capital. McLoughlin started his working life with the now-defunct *Bord na gCapall* (Horse Board) and he also shod horses for the Irish Army before joining Vincent O'Brien in 1985. He admits that Istabraq's feet have tested him to the limit:

> The basic problem is that he has flat feet and while he is not an over-big horse, he is heavy. The front of his hooves have a tendency to look long and every three weeks he has to be reshod. By that stage the hooves really do look as if they need attention and his feet look even flatter than usual. I do what we call 'back, back, the toes'. This means shaving away the bottom of the hoof and taking as much as I dare off the toe. But because he doesn't have straightforward feet, I can't shave off all I would like. When the feet get really bad I don't use bar shoes, as they did at John Gosden's, but I put on stick-on shoes. These mean I don't have to put nails into the hoof and that I can take a little bit more off the bottom.

A week before Christmas John Durkan was allowed to fly back to Ireland and he went to Leopardstown on 27 December to see Istabraq run in the 1st Choice Novice Hurdle over two and a quarter miles. For a man suffering from a supposedly incurable disease and who had been under-going chemotherapy, he looked remarkably well. He did, however, wear a peaked cap to conceal the hair loss. He was thrilled to see many of his old friends and to be at one of the best Irish race meetings of the year. He was also overjoyed by the success of the horse he had tipped for the top. The race was a formality for Istabraq – he started at 100–30 on, with Palette second favourite and the other three runners almost ignored in the market. They were ignored in the race too, with Swan oozing confidence from every pore. The official five and a half length margin –

Palette was again the runner-up – belied the ease with which the favourite won. Had Swan pressed the button in earnest, he could have won by three times as far. Little wonder that Durkan was grinning from ear to ear in the winner's enclosure.

It was his one moment of real happiness before he braced himself for the return to New York four days later. Soon after his arrival at Sloan Kettering, the doctors began making preparations for a bone marrow transplant. As leukaemia has such an effect on the marrow, this is often an essential part of any treatment. It involves extracting marrow from a donor with a syringe and injecting it into the veins of the patient. The donor, however, has to be genetically near-identical and this often means a close relation. The doctors established that two of John's brothers, Aidan and Neil, would have the exact type of marrow for the transplant to succeed. It was agreed that Aidan, who is Bill and Beatrice's youngest child and who closely resembles John in both appearance and character, would be the donor, while Neil would give blood for the transfusion, or rather the platelets which are the clotting agents in the blood. The operation was fixed for Thursday, 13 March.

Istabraq's fourth race over hurdles and his last before Cheltenham, was the Deloitte and Touche Novice Hurdle over two and a quarter miles at Leopardstown on 2 February. It was the day of the Hennessy Cognac Gold Cup when Danoli, Ireland's favourite racehorse, had the huge crowd almost lifting the roof off the stands as they willed him to beat Jodami and Imperial Call. It was also the day of some important Cheltenham trials with Commanche Court winning the opener en route to his Triumph Hurdle victory and Dorans Pride (third in the following month's Cheltenham Gold Cup) landing the Scalp Novice Chase in the hands of the unfortunate Shane Broderick.

Istabraq started at 11–4 on and one of the two joint second favourites was Palette. But it was the little considered Finnegan's Hollow, also owned by McManus and trained by O'Brien, who was to pose problems for the favourite. Things went wrong for Istabraq from the off. He was caught flat-footed when the starter released the tape and he made uncharacteristic mistakes at the final two flights. Early on the run-in, he was headed by Finnegan's Hollow and Swan had to really get down to work on Istabraq to beat his stable companion by a head.

'Finnegan's Hollow had a lot of class at that stage in his career, and he was in top form on the day,' said Swan. 'In fact, he was as good then as he had ever been. I gave my lad only one slap down the shoulder but I had to ride him hard to beat Finnegan's Hollow.'

Conor O'Dwyer, in contrast, showed the runner-up the whip only once and he did not hit his mount. He seemed content to ride with hands and heels, and many questioned whether Finnegan's Hollow would not have won if O'Dwyer had applied more pressure. At a Cheltenham forum in Cork just over a month later, O'Brien was questioned about this race by journalist Alastair Down, the chairman of the panel, and by a particularly persistent member of the 900-strong audience. Not satisfied with the answers secured by Down, the questioner wanted to know what orders O'Brien had given O'Dwyer. The Ballydoyle trainer is a serious individual who has learnt the hard way to be careful about what he says in public, but that evening he brought the house down with his explanation: 'I told Conor to track Istabraq and arrive at the last. But I didn't say anymore and nothing about what he was to do then.'

The Deloitte and Touche result saw Istabraq made a warm favourite for the SunAlliance Hurdle with Finnegan's Hollow high up in the betting for the Citroen Supreme Novices Hurdle, but eleven days before the Cheltenham festival O'Brien caused a flurry of fear in the ante-post markets by issuing a warning that no decision had been made about which races the two horses would go for:

> At the beginning of that season I thought Finnegan's Hollow would win the Champion Hurdle, but he burst a blood vessel on his hurdling début at Navan in November, and we had to go back to square one with him. On his day he was brilliant, but he had a lot of problems with his back, and we probably never got the best out of him. Istabraq had improved all season, and on the Tuesday in the week before the festival he worked better than he had ever done. He went a mile and a half, tucked in behind a lead horse, before quickening past him in fine style. Which race the pair was to run in was JP's decision.

John Patrick McManus was born in Dublin in the week of the 1951 Cheltenham festival. He was twenty-three when he went to the meeting for the first time, and it has had top priority in both his agenda and his objectives ever since, but his family background is far removed from the glamour of the racecourse. His father came from the small County Roscommon town of Arigna but Johnny McManus decided that the local coalmine, where two of his brothers worked, was not the place for him. He found work in Dublin and then in Ballygar in County Galway before moving to Limerick where he ran a plant-hire business and bought a small mixed farm.

The eldest of Johnny McManus's five children became hooked on gambling. He has vivid memories of Merryman II's Grand National win in 1960, and the following year he backed O'Malley Point who was third at 100–6. Half-a-crown each way on Owen's Sedge at 15–2 in the 1963 Leopardstown Chase proved more rewarding. It was the betting rather than the horses that enthralled the boy; racing was simply the means to the end, and it was gambling that led to his downfall in his final few weeks at the Sexton Street Christian Brothers School. On the day of the history exam in his leaving certificate, he fancied a horse running at Limerick racecourse. The exam started at 2.30 pm and nobody was allowed to leave the room for the first twenty minutes. McManus knew he had a tight schedule – after forty-five minutes, one of the brothers would take up position at the door to ensure none of the pupils attempted to leave early – but he managed to slip out and cycle as fast as he could to the racecourse. He had not, however, allowed quite enough time. Just as he reached the course, the race started – and he watched in horror the horse he was going to back streak home in front. He also failed the exam.

He began working for his father, driving a bulldozer for a tenner a week. When the time came for the next eldest, Kevin, to leave school, JP informed his father that the business was not going to be big enough for both of them. McManus senior replied: 'I've got news for you, JP. It's going to be for all five of you.' The eldest son decided it was time to branch out on his own and he was only twenty when he took out a book-maker's licence. He had very little capital and twice he ran out of money, only for his mother to give him a loan to put him back in business.

The lessons that McManus had failed to learn in the classroom were picked up on the racecourse as he observed the betting habits of his colleagues in the ring, and of the punters who were both the customers and the opposition. He came to the conclusion that most bookmakers were no more than glorified punters and that they were apt to panic when they were losing money. They would reduce their margins to try to recover their losses and JP discovered that the value would then lie with the punter. McManus also learned the importance of not trying to recoup those losses too quickly and of waiting for the right moments to do so. He soon became both a punter and a bookmaker.

It was when he began owning horses, starting with Cill Dara who won the 1977 Irish Cesarewitch for him, that his name became known, feared and eventually revered. He liked to back his horses when they were going for the races he thought they could win, and he soon singled out the National Hunt Chase as a principal target. He reckoned that the four mile race, confined to amateurs, was the weakest in the National Hunt festival in terms of class and therefore the easiest to win, and in 1978 he ran Jack Of Trumps. The horse started odds-on and McManus, just back from his honeymoon, eventually decided that the price was too short for him to risk his money. It was just as well because the horse fell. McManus was not so lucky in the race the following year when his National Hunt Chase runner was Deep Gale. He was convinced he was on a roll after he had had £2000 at 20–1 on Master Smudge in the SunAlliance Chase on the opening day, and the outsider had come home in front. He had already planned to have a big bet on Deep Gale, and he added to his stake everything he got back from the bookies on Master Smudge. His bet was enough to bring down the favourite's price from 2–1 to 11–10. In their more reflective moments, big-time gamblers will sometimes say that a bet only really moves them when it is so big that it is more than they can afford to lose. McManus is a modest man who seldom talks about the size of his winnings and his losses, for fear of sounding brash, but in 1979 his wealth was only a fraction of what it is today and a stake of nearly £50,000 was such a bet for him. Deep Gale was travelling well for most of the four miles and he was just beginning to close on the leaders when he fell at the nineteenth.

The owner's addiction to the race was shaken, but it soon continued. In 1983 he ran Bit Of A Skite, fully intending to get back all he had lost on Deep Gale, plus interest for the four intervening years. Shortly before the race, however, when he was assessing the opposition and trying to work out how much the Edward O'Grady-trained seven-year-old had in hand, he came to the conclusion that there were too many ifs and buts to warrant having a bet at all. The bookmakers, finding that the anticipated avalanche of McManus money had not materialised, allowed the horse to drift from 3–1 to 5–1, and he won by four lengths. As his reputation spread – eloquent sports journalist Hugh McIlvanney added to it by nicknaming him The Sundance Kid – McManus ran into problems getting his money on, even at Cheltenham where the market is the strongest of the year. Many refused to take his money, as did several of their colleagues who were frightened of being hit by a man rightly regarded as a professional gambler. McManus became limited to a small number of brave bookmakers, and even then he often had difficulty in being accommodated. In 1994, when he ran Time For A Run in the Coral Cup, he instructed one of his brothers to put the money on for him, but the bet had to be at 10–1 or better; McManus was not prepared to take a shorter price than he felt the horse's chance merited. From his box in the stands, he watched the prices on the betting indicator board on the other side of the straight. These showed 11–1 at the off and as the runners streamed past the stands, he made a quick mental calculation of his possible winnings. Only when the race was at the halfway stage, when his brother finally made it through the crowds to the box, did he discover that he had no bet. The only bookmakers prepared to deal with McManus's brother would offer no better than 8–1. In a manner reminiscent of Limerick all those years earlier, the horse won.

The scale of McManus's racing operation has increased with his wealth and the growth of his business interests. He gave up being a bookmaker ten years ago. It struck him, watching Kevin operating his pitch, how much patience his brother had. JP's patience, when it came to taking small bets on minor races and at minor meetings, was wearing thin. He wanted to move on to bigger things. He became increasingly involved in the financial markets. They provided a new form of gambling for McManus, who found he could deal in huge sums without having limits imposed on him. He moved from his well-appointed stud and comfortable home at Martinstown in County Limerick to Geneva to concentrate on his new operation. He became involved in other ventures, including the luxurious Sandy Lane Hotel in Barbados. He has been able to plough more money into horses and he has nearly a hundred in training, mostly in Ireland. He flies back to see them run as often as he can, and he usually arrives at the racecourse by helicopter. It is his one sign of ostentation and it is done to save time, not to make an impression. He dislikes talking about his wealth, his appearances in the gossip columns are made with reluctance on his part, and are usually in connection with a charity event. He gives generously to what he considers worthwhile causes, and he recently offered to contribute £50 million for a new national stadium in Ireland; he must have had second thoughts when he became the target of comment and criticism in some sections of the media who seemed convinced that there must be a hidden reason for his 'no strings attached' generosity. However, in racing, where reputations invariably suffer from jealousy, back-biting and sometimes spite, few people have a bad word for him. This is all the more remarkable, given his gambling instincts, but even in the ring he is regarded as a gentleman.

The way he dealt with the Finnegan's Hollow-Istabraq issue was typical of the man. Although Aidan O'Brien said it was his decision, that is not how McManus viewed it. His approach is to sit down with those involved, in this case the Ballydoyle trainer and his jockey, and discuss the alternatives. Although he refrained from making it an issue, it went against the grain to run two fancied horses in the same race. What also weighed on his mind was that Christy Roche, at the time O'Brien's stable jockey on the Flat, had ridden Istabraq in some of his work and had given his opinion that this was a two-mile horse over hurdles. Roche, now one of McManus's main trainers, was seven times Ireland's champion Flat jockey and known to be a particularly shrewd judge of a horse. In the end, though, logic suggested that Istabraq, having stayed so well on the Flat, should go for the longer race, particularly as all three men recalled John Durkan's prediction. However, the nearest McManus got to making a decision or even exercising his casting vote, was to say: 'Well, Aidan, if you think Finnegan's Hollow is right for the Supreme Novices, and if Charlie thinks so too, perhaps we should run Istabraq in the SunAlliance.'

6 SunAlliance Glory

Aidan O'Brien had trained his first Cheltenham winner the previous year when Urubande made much of the running in the Sun Alliance Hurdle. Mentally he was a far tougher horse than Istabraq who was still showing a tendency to fret whenever he was asked to do anything out of the ordinary at home, and O'Brien wondered whether he should wait until the morning of the race before flying him to Cheltenham. He knew that there is a strong argument to be made for keeping a horse in his own stable the night before a big race. It is what the horse is used to – Istabraq is far from alone in being upset by changes in routine – and the trip was relatively easy to make, a short journey to Shannon airport for a straightforward direct flight. Although most Irish Cheltenham runners fly to Bristol, there is an airport at Staverton, little more than three miles from the course. Travelling can be just as tiring for horses as it is for human beings, and they too suffer from jetlag. But, as with some athletes, many racehorses can perform right up to their best almost straight off the plane. O'Brien knew that it was the practice of Edward O'Grady to fly the brilliant chaser Sound Man from Tipperary for big races in England first thing in the morning and fly the horse home the same evening. Indeed, O'Brien had sometimes done this with his Flat horses. It was not until the 1998 Derby that he was forced to concede that the risks of delay were too great. That day the incoming plane was held up by fog at Shannon to such an extent that the horsebox, laid on to take the three O'Brien runners on the final leg of their journey to Epsom, had to be given a police escort to get it there on time. O'Brien was worried how the nervous Istabraq would react to a night in the race-course stables. If he did not eat or sleep, he would be in no condition to give of his best in the race. However, even without the Derby example to guide him, the trainer was uncomfortably aware of the risks he would be running if he waited until the morning of the race. He came to the conclusion that these were risks he dare not run, no matter how stressed Istabraq might become.

McManus had ten runners at the meeting in his emerald green and orange hooped colours, taken from the South Liberties hurling club of which he was chairman in the early 1970s. Finnegan's Hollow in the Citroen Supreme Novices Hurdle was the first of them. The gelding's owner, influenced by the Deloitte and Touche, and by O'Brien's reports of the horse's subsequent work, was convinced Finnegan's Hollow had a winning chance. He went for a big bet – he says he cannot remember how much he had on (his usual answer when pressed on the size of his gambles) – and the horse started 2–1 favourite in a field of sixteen. He looked like winning when Charlie Swan – 'I have never been travelling so easily coming down the hill at Cheltenham as I was then' – swept him into the lead approaching the third last. Finnegan's Hollow did not judge it quite right, probably because he was galloping downhill, and he got in a bit too close. He hit the hurdle, not hard, but enough to unbalance him when he landed, with his hindquarters a bit higher in the air than would normally have been the case. The weight of his quarters and the impetus of well over 30mph proved too much for his front legs and they buckled. Finnegan's Hollow crashed to the ground, pitching Swan hard into the turf. The jockey felt sick, not because of the jarring impact, or because he had come perilously close to being injured by the horses behind, but because he had been so sure he was going to win.

McManus, whose polite smile is the same whether he wins or loses, shrugged off the loss of his bet. He was more concerned about having lost what he regarded as one of his best chances of winning a race at that year's Cheltenham festival. Others found it harder to disguise the loss of their cash. McManus invites a large group of friends to his box each year. Some are famous hurlers of the South Liberties era, others are high-powered businessmen who are involved with him in financial dealings. McManus might well take a lead from them in his business transactions but when it comes to horses and gambling on them, the businessmen take JP's lead. If he backed one of his, they wanted their money on too. Almost all of them had plunged heavily on Finnegan's Hollow. When Charlie Swan went up to the box at the end of racing that day, he detected an air of gloom and he realised why. When a number of them said 'I hope you do it tomorrow,' he knew they intended to get their money back on Istabraq.

Swan, who normally manages a cheerful smile no matter how badly things have gone, drove to the Cheltenham home of Ranulph and Hope Middleton a worried man. 'I just hope this Istabraq wins tomorrow,' he muttered to his wife Tina. Swan's worry turned to foreboding the next day when he watched the Channel 4 *Morning Line* programme and heard Ted Walsh and John McCririck sparring over the horse's chances. McCririck asked the outspoken Irish pundit if he would put his last £40,000 on the horse. 'Yes, I would,' came the unhesitating reply. 'I would also mortgage my house and put on another £40,000.'

Unusually, there had been no Irish winner on the first day and the Royal SunAlliance Novices Hurdle (the sponsors changed the race's title three times in as many years) was the first race on the second. Swan's mood was not improved on reaching the weighing room, where several of his English-based rivals began pulling his leg. 'You'd better win on this one, Charlie,' they said. 'The whole of Ireland's backing him, half England too.'

Swan knew only too well that several of the opposition had solid claims. Royaltino, trained in France by Francois Doumen, had won at Enghien and Auteuil, before proving his ability by beating some decent opposition over the SunAlliance trip at Kempton. Agistment had won all his three hurdle starts for Jimmy Fitzgerald and was ridden by the stylish Richard Dunwoody. Mighty Moss had won his first two hurdle races and finished second in his other three; and Forest Ivory had won his first two starts before running Agistment to a neck on his final outing.

The big crowd at Cheltenham, particularly the portion milling round the already busy bookmakers' ring, was buzzing in anticipation. Across the Atlantic, the sense of excitement was every bit as great, at least in one ward of the Sloan Kettering Hospital. John Durkan had adopted a courageously positive attitude about his illness ever since the implications had first been spelt out to him by the doctors at St Vincent's. Despite the odds being stacked against him, he was convinced he would overcome the disease, make a full recovery and achieve his ambition of becoming a trainer. Carol, encouraged by her husband's convictions, shared his belief, and so did his mother. Only Bill Durkan, told by the doctors early on that in reality his son had little chance, felt differently – and he kept his views to himself. John was also buoyed up by the telephone calls he repeatedly received from his racing friends.

It is possible to obtain a link-up to the Satellite Information Services racing coverage, which is what is shown in the betting shops, in many parts of the world but John found, much to his disappointment, that he was unable to get either this or a radio commentary in the hospital. Nor could either be arranged in the Central Park apartment. Instead Carol arranged to have the commentary relayed to him via her father's mobile. John had been looking forward to Cheltenham for weeks, and in particular to Istabraq's race. The fact that he was due to have the bone marrow transplant the following day did not spoil his enjoyment. If anything, the opposite. He was convinced the transplant would put him on the road to recovery and bring forward the day when he would be well enough to train the horse himself.

The SunAlliance Hurdle was due off at 2.00 pm, and by 1.30 pm Aidan O'Brien and his staff knew they had problems. The horse who Durkan had warned was 'a bit of a fretter' was showing ominous signs of nerves. Horses tend to become excited when they go to the races; they are bred to race, and most of them love doing it, but once they have experienced a race, they know what is coming. The adrenalin flows and provided it does not overflow or begin too early, it helps their performance. With Istabraq that day, though, it was much more than just adrenalin. He could detect that this race was going to be something special from the attention being paid to all the other horses around him in the racecourse stables, from the sense of pressure and tension which horses are quick to pick up, and above all from the noise of the public address system. For the past two hours interviews on Festival Radio, and other more direct announcements had been clearly heard in the racecourse stables.

Any trainer worth his salt is able to read a horse's mind and Aidan O'Brien is a brilliant equine psychologist. He talked quietly to Istabraq and tried to reassure him, as he put on Swan's saddle, brushed a few specks of dust off the horse's hooves and then gently pushed a water-soaked sponge against his mouth to ease any dryness in the throat. The stable staff led Istabraq out of the yard and along the tarmac walkway which leads behind the weighing room building towards the paddock. But Istabraq, far from being calmed down by finally being on the move, became even more on edge when he saw the other horses and the crowds packed several deep around the parade ring. Nobody quite knows whether the people, the occasion or the noise unsettle a horse most, but in none of his previous races had Istabraq encountered either such a big crowd or so much noise in the paddock. He started to jig about on his toes and to sweat.

Charlie Swan, his own nerves on edge, came out of the weighing room with the other jockeys and searched for O'Brien and McManus. As he walked across the grass towards them, he caught sight of Istabraq and his heart sank. There was sweat on the horse's neck and more showing beneath the saddle. 'He's got very uptight,' said O'Brien with masterly understatement. Swan, looking anxiously across at Istabraq, said that the minute he got up on the horse, he would take him straight down to the start. This is not allowed. The horses have to be led round the paddock with their jockeys on until such time as an official gives the instruction for them to make their way to the start. They normally circle the paddock at least once, to give the public a chance to see them.

When the bell is rung to signal that the jockeys should mount, those leading the horses have to stop where they are. Istabraq was the one closest to the exit. O'Brien legged up Swan and led Istabraq down the chute through the crowd and on to the racecourse, saying 'Try to get him relaxed when you get him down to the start, Charlie.' The runners are meant to make their way there via the strip of all-weather surface that runs alongside the course in order to save the grass. Swan broke this rule too, much to the fury of a white-coated attendant who bellowed at him to get on to the all-weather surface. Istabraq was by now caked in sweat from his neck to his girth.

The bookmakers, determined to take no chances with a horse that JP McManus seemed certain to back, had opened Istabraq at 11–10 but, when they saw what a bag of nerves he had become, they marked him out to 11–8. Yet the sheer volume of money for the favourite forced them to cut him to 6–5. A hefty slice of that money belonged to McManus who, with the previous day's losses to recover, had given his instructions to those putting it on for him when the horse was still in the paddock. Had he seen how much worse the sweating had become by the time Istabraq reached the course, he would have made a hasty call on his mobile. But Channel 4 asked him to do a brief interview before he left the parade ring and so it was not until he reached his box that he learned the worst. By that time the money was on and, he feared, lost.

Swan, down at the start several minutes before the others arrived, walked his mount towards one of the inspection hurdles and halted him in front of it. Istabraq stood still and began to look round him, with his ears pricked. There was no sign of any other horses or people. There was also no noise and he began to relax. Then the other runners came galloping up, the few moments of peace were forgotten and the sweating started again. Swan, sensing that he had to give the horse something else to think about, broke him into a canter to show him the first hurdle. Several of the other jockeys did the same. They all returned to the start and the starter began his roll call of the jockeys to make doubly sure they had all arrived. Swan was a worried man. It was all too obvious that the horse was still very uptight. The starter called out to the jockeys to line up and Istabraq, covered in a white lather, leapt forward and charged at the tape. Swan only just succeeded in stopping him bursting through and causing a false start. The jockey's mind, working overtime ever since he first arrived in the paddock, registered a last-gasp solution:

> My plan all along had been to ride him handy, close up behind
> the leaders, but the way he charged the tape convinced me that

he would run keen and much too free. I decided I would jump off slower and then try to relax him. When the tape went up, he was caught a little bit flat-footed. That was a big help because most of the others were now in front and I was able to tuck him in behind. Going past the stands we were last and, most important of all, he had settled.

John Durkan, mobile to his ear and with Carol on the bed beside him also listening in, could not hear Istabraq's name. When he did, he could not understand why the horse was not up with the leaders. The way to ride him, as Willie Carson and Pat Eddery had proved, was from the front. Then he heard the commentator say 'and Istabraq is last of all'. Durkan swore loudly, threw the phone down on the bed and said despairingly, 'he can't win from there'. Carol picked up the phone and put it to her ear. Seconds later she selflessly handed it back to her husband.

Swan continued to bide his time at the back of the field as the sixteen remaining horses – the unfortunate Agistment had fallen heavily at the first, broken his neck and was dead – swept along the back straight and up the hill to the highest point of the course. He knew he was much too far back, but he was convinced that his last lingering hopes would be swept away if he attempted to make ground going uphill. Just at the top of the hill, though, he started to squeeze with his legs. Istabraq, the nerves forgotten, was concentrating on racing and for the first time in hours was enjoying himself. He took the hurdle cleanly and landed running. The next was the third from home and once over it Swan began pushing. He still was not sure that he had enough in the tank for the final climb to the post – all that sweating must have sapped the horse's energy to the tune of several lengths – but like Carson before him, he had come to the conclusion that Istabraq did not do anything in a hurry. The going, officially good to firm, was very fast and Swan was convinced that Istabraq would not be able to accelerate on it, even if he had enough left to do so. He wanted, therefore, to be on the heels of the leaders by the time they turned for home.

Istabraq, by now in his element, somehow found a whole lot more and Swan was able to get him back on the bridle before he reached the second last. There were three horses in front of him, but Istabraq was travelling as strongly as any of them and his jockey did not want to check his momentum. He therefore had to look for room to get past them. His instinct was to pass on the outside; there is an unwritten rule among jockeys that anybody who attempts to overtake on the inner is asking for trouble and deserves what he gets. But Forest Ivory, ridden by Richard Johnson, was too far wide for Swan to pass on his outside. He decided to head for a gap between Forest Ivory and Daraydan on whom young Flat race jockey Richard Hughes was having one of the thrills of his life. Swan, three-quarters of a length behind as he went towards the hurdle at a ferocious pace, kicked his mount. He wanted to be upsides or as near level as possible when he jumped. Istabraq responded bravely but as he took off, Forest Ivory veered to the left and cannoned into him.

When a horse is bumped in mid-air and travelling at over 30mph, he is going to have the devil's own job keeping his footing when he lands. Istabraq's head nodded dangerously as his feet touched the ground and Swan, uttering a brief but silent and heartfelt plea to the Almighty, sat like a limpet as he felt the horse's legs slipping from under him. Somehow Istabraq managed to stay upright, but he had been partially winded by the bump. Swan gave him three strides to recover and then started riding. He could hardly believe it when he felt the horse responding and by the time he reached the last he was just in front.

Having got so far and survived so much, Swan was determined not to be denied but Fred Hutsby on Mighty Moss felt just the same. Hutsby was only twenty and had ridden his first winner, on Mighty Moss, just fifteen months earlier. He had ridden in only seventeen races under rules and was not allowed to claim his 7lb allowance. He was effectively putting up 7lb overweight. Several racing journalists had been critical of both his ability and his style and some had suggested that his father should put up a proper jockey. But young Hutsby had done everything right and far from panicking through inexperience, the amateur settled down to fight it out with the famous Irish champion. Swan repeatedly asked Istabraq for more and Hutsby matched him every time. Both horses kept responding, and while the narrow advantage that Istabraq had gained at the last was not reduced, it was not increased either. It was only by a length that he held on, with Swan standing up in the irons and turning to wave his whip in the direction of the McManus box. JP, having his back slapped and his hand shaken, was close to tears. He had recovered his Finnegan's Hollow losses but that, as he admitted afterwards, had nothing to do with it. What mattered was that his horse had won and had triumphed over all the adversity of the previous thirty minutes.

Irish winners at Cheltenham are traditionally given the sort of noisy reception that is seen elsewhere only with the likes of the winning goal in a cup final. As many of the visiting punters had followed the McManus example by plunging on the favourite, Istabraq made his way into the amphitheatre-like winner's enclosure with tumultuous cheers echoing through the stands. Hordes of over-enthusiastic racegoers burst their way past the officials who found themselves powerless to stem the tide. Edward Gillespie, the course's long-serving and normally good-humoured managing director, had feared just such a pitch invasion if Danoli won the following day's Gold Cup, and he had made plans to keep the crowds at bay. He was not prepared for it twenty-four hours earlier, and when he saw what he thought was a particularly unruly racegoer vaulting over the railings into the winner's enclosure, he marched up and ordered him out. Several of the onlookers started to boo and Swan, turning to see what the disturbance was all about, thought that the ecstatic Irish were welcoming the runner-up! Only when the taunts finally registered did Gillespie realise that he had nabbed one of the heroes of the hour. Aidan O'Brien, used to the more casual approach to badges in his native country, had handed his to someone who he thought would appreciate it more. Gillespie promptly apologised, but the story of his gaffe is likely to haunt him for as long as O'Brien goes on making headlines.

John Durkan, every bit as excited as anybody at Cheltenham, continued to listen in as his father-in-law relayed what was happening, and the phone was passed to McManus, Swan and O'Brien for each to be congratulated and for them to wish the patient well. 'I said well done to him,' said O'Brien. 'I knew what a bad way he was in and that Istabraq winning meant a lot to him. He had made a big statement saying that the horse would win at Cheltenham and he had been proved right. I said that to him too.'

The doctors in the Sloan Kettering Hospital were more concerned about what was to happen the following day and what they should do about the drama that was unfolding around them. Aidan Durkan had arrived in New York in good spirits, delighted to be doing his bit to save his brother's life, but on the morning of the SunAlliance Hurdle he felt unwell. When he reached the hospital, he was feeling feverish and he had a nasty suspicion he was running a temperature. This was promptly confirmed, and the doctors diagnosed a flu-like virus. He would obviously be alright in a few days but everything was in place for the transplant the next day. After much discussion, it was decided to proceed but with Neil Durkan stepping in to give the marrow. Blood taken from Aidan previously would be used for the platelets. Aidan was upset, he felt it was his marrow that should be used. Even today, he openly wonders whether things might have been different if he had not fallen ill on that fateful day.

7 Black Clouds

T he obvious next race for a SunAlliance Hurdle winner is the Martell Aintree Hurdle on Grand National day. It provides a valuable opportunity for the top staying novices to be tested against Champion Hurdle horses, with the distance (two and a half miles) often compensating the novices for the big step up in class. In 1994 Danoli had won both races, beating Champion Hurdle winner Flakey Dove into a remote fifth at Aintree. Two years later Urubande had repeated the performance. The race was run three and a half weeks after Cheltenham in 1997, enough time for a horse with a reasonably tough constitution to recover, although two cross-channel flights inside a month would be demanding for any horse. O'Brien discussed the situation with McManus and Swan. The owner, in particular, felt that Cheltenham had been an exhausting experience for Istabraq and that it would be prudent to keep him to races in Ireland for the remainder of the season. He felt the same about Finnegan's Hollow after his heavy fall. It was agreed that both would run at the Fairyhouse Easter meeting at the beginning of Aintree week.

O'Brien decided to send Urubande for the Martell Aintree Hurdle instead, but he had lost his form and he finished a distant fifth. Make A Stand, who had galloped the opposition into the ground in the Champion Hurdle, was also well beaten. Shortly after the race was run, the course had to be evacuated as a result of an IRA bomb scare that resulted in the Grand National being delayed until 5.00 pm the following Monday. The effect on Istabraq's delicate mental make-up of all the consternation, had he been there, can only be imagined.

It was decided that Finnegan's Hollow should run in the £20,000

Jameson Gold Cup Novice Hurdle over two miles on Easter Monday and that Istabraq would be kept for the £10,000 Festival Novice Hurdle over half a mile further two days later. Finnegan's Hollow started at 7–4 on, but he was beaten a long way out and finished lame; he was never the same again after that Cheltenham fall and he has not won since. Istabraq did not run at Fairyhouse. O'Brien came to the conclusion that the race was too soon after the horse's Cheltenham experience and that it would be better to wait for the £30,000 Stanley Cooker Champion Novice Hurdle over the same trip at Punchestown three weeks later. But O'Brien and Swan still won the Fairyhouse race, with Moscow Express.

Punchestown came six weeks after John Durkan's bone marrow transplant, and on the first day of the meeting JP McManus rang the Sloan Kettering Hospital. The transplant had gone smoothly, despite the alarm over the switch of donor, but Durkan was becoming increasingly concerned that there appeared to be no improvement in his health. If anything, he felt worse than before the transplant. However, he was still sure he would make a full recovery and he did his best to hide his concerns when he spoke to Istabraq's owner. He said he expected to be in the hospital for a further two months and then return home. He asked about the Punchestown race and the strength of the opposition before wishing McManus luck. On paper Istabraq had little to beat. The only serious rival, according to the betting, was the David Nicholson-trained Soldat who had run in the SunAlliance despite being only a four-year-old; but he had been beaten nearly twelve lengths into fifth. Glebe Lad was a course winner who had won by four lengths on his most recent start, but he was not to achieve his full potential until he was sent over fences – he won the Irish Grand National two years later. Istabraq's biggest problem was expected to be his nerves. Would his return to the racecourse bring the Cheltenham memories flooding back? Would he worry that he was going to have another hard race? Would he again get himself in such a state that he would be awash with sweat by the time he got out onto the course?

Aidan O'Brien and Charlie Swan, aware more than most of these imponderables, decided to take no chances. Istabraq was brought into the parade ring late and Swan took him almost straight off down to the start, ignoring the instruction of the clerk of the course, Joe Collins, that he should make a full circuit of the paddock. The horse was in public view just long enough for those wanting to back him to see that there was not the slightest sign of nerves, not even a trace of sweat, and the bookmakers were forced to cut their opening offer of 1–2 to 4–11. In other words, if you wanted to win £400, you had to put on £1100 and that was before taking into account the betting tax – five per cent on the course and ten per cent in the Irish betting shops. The bookmakers were effectively saying that they did not want to bet against Istabraq. It was to be the first of many such occasions in the horse's jumping career.

He travelled like a certainty all the way. Although he made a mistake at the fourth last hurdle and a lesser one at the next, he was never in the slightest danger and he cruised home nine lengths in front of Soldat, despite Swan starting to pull up well before the line. The crowd cheered him home. Not many had been bold enough to back him – Irish punters tend not to bet on horses that start odds-on – but they recognised a brilliant performance and they wanted to show their appreciation. They did it again when he returned to the winner's enclosure. But the trainer and the jockey were in trouble. The latter had been reported to the stewards by the clerk of the course for disobeying his instruction. Swan was fined £200 and he was warned that he should comply with the orders of officials in future. O'Brien was fined the same amount for bringing Istabraq into the parade ring so late.

This was Istabraq's sixth race of the season and it had already been decided that he should not run again until the autumn. Suggestions came from some of the press that the horse might go for the French Champion Hurdle or run on the Flat. But McManus pointed out that racing on the level held little appeal for him, and in any case he felt the horse had done enough for one season. The question for the next season was which direction would he take? Would he do the logical thing and step up in distance to the extended three miles of the Stayers' Hurdle or take the brave route and go for the Champion? O'Brien, who seldom shirks a challenge when he thinks a horse is good enough, favoured the latter. Indeed he had even entered the horse for the 1997 Champion Hurdle, but the jockey did not agree, saying: 'I was convinced he was a stayer, not a two-mile horse, because he stayed so well on the Flat, and he was the same over hurdles.' No winner of the SunAlliance Hurdle had ever gone on to win the Champion, basically because a horse who stays well enough to win over two miles and five furlongs as a novice does not have the speed to beat the best over two miles. The bookmakers, not noted for their generosity, quoted Istabraq at 14–1 for the 1998 Champion Hurdle. They had few takers.

Istabraq, taken back to Ballydoyle, was given a few weeks to wind down before being sent to McManus's Martinstown Stud, outside the small town of Kilmallock, for the first of his summer holidays. He was turned out into a paddock, day and night, with a companion, Mister Donovan, who had won the Sun Alliance Hurdle in the McManus colours fifteen years earlier. There was no holiday for Aidan O'Brien though. He was busy writing his name into the record books on the Flat, winning the first three Irish classics and producing a brilliant two-year-old named King Of Kings.

At the beginning of May, Beatrice Durkan left New York to return to Ireland. She had misgivings about leaving her son, but she felt she had to spend some time with the rest of her family. A month later, however, she was back at the hospital where the patient's progress, or rather lack of progress, was causing considerable concern. The bone marrow transplant had not had the desired effect. Indeed, John's body was showing signs of rejecting the new marrow and he had developed lymphoma (cancer of the lymph glands). He had to have an emergency operation and his hopes of an early return to Ireland were dashed. The pain, suffering and misery he endured can be imagined; but his wife, who was undergoing considerable mental torment at seeing the man she loved suffer so much, was struck by how little he complained. The fax messages from Camas Park continued, as did the telephone calls from his friends. Eddie Hales and Jamie Osborne both flew to New York to visit him.

John had still not given up hope of making a full recovery and Carol, gaining strength from her husband's positive attitude, felt he would conquer both the leukaemia and the lymphoma. Earlier in the year he had spent quite a bit of his time in the Central Park apartment, going into the hospital for tests, treatment and examinations, then returning to the apartment for a few days at a time. But after the operation the length of his stays in hospital increased and he was allowed out only now and again. Even so, he talked often to his mother about returning to Ireland and he began to make plans for a flying visit. Just as he and Beatrice felt he would soon be ready to make the trip, further tests revealed a low bloodcount and he was told he would have to stay in the hospital. His mother detected an increasing anxiety, and one dark day John confided to her that he felt he would 'never see the sky over Ireland again'.

He developed a particular rapport with the doctor in charge of his case, Grace Popadopolis, and he would often chat to her at length. In September 1997, when he was having one of his regular discussions with her, he had a blackout. There was no warning; he had been sitting on the bed talking to the doctor quite normally when it happened. He was unconscious for about two minutes. Doctor Popadopolis and her colleagues decided he should have a brain scan which revealed a cancerous spot on the brain. There was no question of an early return.

The National Hunt horses at Ballydoyle are stabled in a group of nine boxes, well away from the Flat horses in the main yard which was built at the side of Vincent O'Brien's house, and on the other side of the estate from the two-year-olds. These are housed in the stables where David O'Brien used to train. His father used to keep a few foals and yearlings in the nine-box yard and these were looked after by Margo Cooke who lived in the small house beside it. The yard became known as Margo's Yard and the name has remained even though she retired in 1997. Her place was taken by Anita Harvey, a pleasant dark-haired young woman who comes from Inver in County Donegal where her father works on a fish farm. She grew up with a fascination for horses and she soon found the local riding school a compelling attraction. But racehorses interested her even more, and after school and at weekends she would help out at the nearby yard of trainer PJ McCartan.

On leaving school, she worked for him for two years before joining Ian Duncan at Crumlin in County Antrim. It was during her three and a half years with Duncan that she had her first ride in a race. Her second did not come until July 1998, when she was twenty-four and rode Symboli Phoenix for Christy Roche in the Ladies Derby at the Curragh. Eleven months earlier she joined Aidan O'Brien at Piltown. It was at the beginning of the following year that she transferred to Ballydoyle to take over Margo's Yard.

She is responsible for feeding Istabraq and the other jumpers. The basic menu is nuts for breakfast, oats at lunchtime and in the evening more nuts. The amount each horse is given depends on how much work they are doing. The more the work is stepped up, the more food they get. 'Istabraq is basically a well-behaved horse and there is normally no trace of any nervousness at home,' says Anita. 'When he gets fit, he becomes very sharp and you know that he is ready to run. So does he and he also knows when he is in the build-up to Cheltenham. I don't normally exercise him, but when I have done I have found him a brilliant horse to ride. He has never once tried anything on.'

Istabraq's lad is Davy Clifford who began looking after the horse soon after the SunAlliance. His uncle Leo works at the Aga Khan's Gilltown Stud near Kilcullen, where Clifford comes from, and where his father works as a painter and decorator after spending twenty-one years in the Irish army. Clifford's ambition was to become a jockey, and after leaving school he started in racing with Michael Halford on the Curragh. When he was unable to pick up even a ride in a race, he moved to Pat Barrett who he hoped would give him opportunities on the racecourse.

However, Clifford, like so many before him, discovered that racing stables are largely staffed by people who once entertained similar unfulfilled aspirations. He joined Jessica Harrington who has a sizeable string of jumpers at Moone, barely twelve miles from Kilcullen. There was still no race-riding and Clifford, by now realising that he was never going to be given the chance to become a jockey, decided to move on. Mrs Harrington, sister of trainer John Fowler and wife of bloodstock agent Johnny Harrington, had good horses but those trained by Aidan O'Brien were better – Clifford's ambitions were centred on associating with the best. He was twenty-five when he moved to Ballydoyle.

There was never much doubt about where Istabraq would start his second season over jumps. McManus, looking through the programmes for the previous year, realised there was no suitable early season race for a high-class hurdler and so he offered to sponsor one. He chose the Tipperary meeting in mid-October and his contribution was big enough to ensure that the two mile conditions hurdle carried a prize of £50,000. He named it the John James McManus Memorial Hurdle in honour of his father and it was agreed that his brother Kevin would present the trophies. Also on the card were more sponsored jump races, including the Kevin McManus Bookmaker Novice Chase and the Kevin McManus Bookmaker Novice Hurdle. The two two-year-old races were named after Mister Donovan and Deep Gale.

However, there were problems with the course. This was to be the richest day's racing Tipperary had staged in its eighty-one-year history, but it had never been able to withstand a lot of rain. The ground was already soft when racecourse manager David Wright telephoned the Met Office for an updated forecast on the day before the meeting. He was horrified to hear that torrential rain was expected that evening, with more of the same forecast for the following morning. He was forced to call a 6.30 am inspection.

Aidan O'Brien was twenty-eight on the day of the race and at Gowran Park the previous day he had sent out his 200th winner of the year. It was an incredible total in a country where there were less than 1800 races, yet in 1995 he had swept aside all previous records by notching up 242 winners.

Tipperary survived both the inspection and the heavy rain, much to David Wright's relief, and McManus was optimistic that Finnegan's Hollow would win the novice chase. It was the horse's first race since his disappointing run at Fairyhouse on Easter Monday, and his first over fences. Sadly, it turned out to be no more than the second instalment of what was to prove a long, downhill slide. He was beaten well before he fell heavily at the last. He fired Charlie Swan into the mud and for ten minutes he lay winded in the pouring rain, before staggering to his feet.

The ground was so bad that two of Istabraq's main opponents, Space Trucker and Grimes, had to be withdrawn. Punting Pete, named by owner Dr Brendan Doyle after his friend Peter McCarthy (son-in-law of Paddy Mullins and later chairman of the Irish Racehorse Owners Association), loved to make the running at a furious pace, but in the testing ground this was a suicidal tactic. The going and the twelve-length lead that he poached early on combined to leave him a spent force by the time he reached the third last. Swan decided to go on with Istabraq and after jumping the next, the horse seemed to find another gear to leave the opposition toiling in his wake. It was an impressive performance, and the bookmakers reacted accordingly. Corals cut Istabraq's Champion Hurdle price from 12–1 to 8–1, while Paddy Power made him joint favourite with Shadow Leader and Make A Stand at 7–1.

Aidan O'Brien promptly spelled out the plan of campaign for the remainder of the season: the Hatton's Grace Hurdle at Fairyhouse, the December Festival Hurdle at Leopardstown, the AIG Europe Champion Hurdle at the same course, and then the Champion itself. However, it was a far from happy birthday for the victorious trainer. His Promalee, starting at 3–1 on for the Kevin McManus Bookmaker Novice Hurdle, was beaten all ends up by the Richard Dunwoody-ridden Go Roger Go (owned by JP), and after the Deep Gale Two-Year-Old Maiden, the stewards had him in over the running of Gentle Thoughts. O'Brien ran four in the race, including 7–4 favourite Dove Orchid who finished second. Gentle Thoughts, ridden by Seamus Heffernan, started joint second favourite and ran on in the closing stages to take third.

The stewards decided that Heffernan had not made sufficient effort and they suspended him for a fortnight. They also ruled that O'Brien had used the racecourse as a training ground and they fined him £500. Gentle Thoughts was suspended for thirty days, which meant that she would not be able to run again until the following season. The fine was insignificant for a man of O'Brien's earning power. His percentage from the four races he won at Tipperary that day amounted to over £4000, but he felt that the stewards had cast doubts on his integrity – using the racecourse as a training ground is often a delicate way of saying that the horse has not been trying. O'Brien decided to lodge an appeal, not just against the fine but against the whole sentence. However, he was only partially successful; the appeal stewards ruled that the fine was wrong, as was the filly's suspension, but they decided that Heffernan's ban should stand.

John Durkan, who had been faxed the press reports of Istabraq's victory, was determined to return to Ireland. His condition had deteriorated. The lymphoma, coupled with the leukaemia, had caused his body to swell. This was particularly noticeable with his face; the clear-cut features were by now almost buried beneath the swelling and touching anything was painful. Not surprisingly, he was becoming increasingly depressed and he was having to have counselling on an almost daily basis. He told the doctors he wanted to go home. They stressed that this would be a mistake. It was important that he stayed in the hospital and continued his treatment. This only made him more depressed. While he still had not given up hope of getting better, he felt he had to get away. If he could only return to Ireland, he might give himself a chance. He talked to Grace Popadopolis once more and impressed on her that he must leave the hospital, if only for a time. The doctor finally relented. She made arrangements for her patient to continue his treatment at St James's Hospital in Dublin under Professor McCann, but she said that she hoped he would return in a few weeks' time. The flight was booked for 4 November. Carol was amazed and delighted at the transformation in her husband.

'Things had not gone well for him in New York and by this stage he was very ill,' she said. 'Life was hell for him and he felt he just couldn't hack it any more in the hospital. But I had never seen him so excited as he was on the day we got on the plane to come home.'

She and John moved into the Durkans' home above Stepaside. Each day he would be driven to St James's Hospital in the centre of Dublin for treatment and each evening he would return to his parents' house. Just under three weeks after his return President Mary McAleese was due to perform the opening ceremony of a Cheshire Home in Bohola and Bill Durkan had been invited to attend. The evening before he asked his son if he would like to go with him, and if he liked they could go on to Knock afterwards. John knew that his father was suggesting he might like to go to the shrine at Knock to pray. He agreed and his father's heart went out to him when he saw his son kneeling in the church.

The Hatton's Grace Hurdle was on the Sunday after the Knock visit and Bill Durkan had already planned to accompany John to Fairyhouse. The two and a half miles was widely believed to be much more in Istabraq's favour than the two miles of the Tipperary race – it was still supposed that the horse needed a trip – and the race looked a formality. There were only five runners and two of them, Cockney Lad and Bolino Star, had been among the opposition at Tipperary; Gazalani had little to recommend him while Blushing Sand had not raced for nearly eight months and he was three stone behind Istabraq on the official handicap ratings. Indeed, these suggested that Istabraq, who started at 3–1 on, had nothing to fear from any of the four with the exception of Cockney Lad who was only 3lb inferior to the favourite.

The Avonmore Waterford Hatton's Grace Hurdle was the fifth race on the card and early in the afternoon John, accompanied by his father, went into the weighing room to meet some of his old friends. They all knew that he had been in America having treatment for leukaemia, but few of them were aware of the lymphoma or just how seriously ill he was. He seemed cheerful, he spoke quite normally and the only real indication that something was wrong was his puffed-up face. He looked as if he was suffering from mumps. He wore gloves, and those walking up to him to shake his hand were surprised to find his father reaching across and grasping the proffered right hand with his own. Bill Durkan gave no reason for doing this nor did he say anything about his son's illness.

Hardly anyone knew that for John to have his hand shaken, no matter how gently, would have caused him almost unbearable pain. None of them were aware that it was taking all his strength just to stand up.

For the first time Swan adopted the tactics that Pat Eddery and Willie Carson had found suited Istabraq best. But the reason he did so was because he thought that none of the other four were going to set a decent pace and a steady one would play into the hands of Cockney Lad and Bolino Star, who both had plenty of speed over two miles. Istabraq was still eight kilos above his ideal racing weight, but apart from a slight mistake at the fourth hurdle, everything went smoothly. Paul Carberry on Cockney Lad moved up threateningly at the second last but immediately after jumping it, Swan glanced back, quickened the tempo and the race was as good as over.

'It was only a Mickey Mouse race, really,' said O'Brien, 'and Istabraq was lazing along in front. In fact, he was now a stronger horse than in his first season.' Charlie Swan at last began to feel that Istabraq might be as effective over the two miles of the Champion Hurdle as he had been over longer trips. What convinced him was that the faster the gallop, the better Istabraq jumped. John Durkan was impressed and he said: 'I always felt that Istabraq would be this good and I now think he can win the Champion provided the ground is on the soft side.'

It was a significant proviso and it was to some extent echoed by one of the big three British bookmaking firms. Simon Clare, son of Professor Anthony Clare (of *In The Psychiatrist's Chair* fame), was representing Corals and he said: 'The ground was in Istabraq's favour here and to my mind this two and a half miles – not the two miles of the Champion Hurdle – is his preferred trip. We already knew that he was a good horse. All this race proved was that he was well.'

Interestingly, Mike Dillon of Ladbrokes took a totally different view, saying: 'I have long believed that what Istabraq needs is two miles on a stiff course and the Hatton's Grace was not run to suit him at all.'

Both Ladbrokes and Hills made Istabraq 5–1 favourite for the Champion Hurdle. Corals made him joint favourite with Shadow Leader at 6–1. None of the three tempted McManus who wryly remarked: 'It's easy to make a horse favourite – the trouble is that this one is favourite without any money going on him.'

8 In Mourning

On their way home, Bill Durkan suggested to his son that they call in to a particular hamburger restaurant. It was a familiar haunt from the days when John was a teenager; he and the other Durkan children would be taken there by their father on the way back from the races, often as part of the celebrations of a Durkan-trained victory. John was excited at the prospect of seeing old faces and disappointed to find the place almost empty. The old crowd had moved on. These were particularly poignant moments for Bill, who was acutely aware that almost everything he was doing with his son was going to be for the last time. He had been told by the doctors at St James's that the cancerous spot on the brain had grown larger and that any last hopes of recovery were now gone.

A week later they went to Knock again, this time at John's suggestion, and again he prayed. It had been decided that he should return to the Sloan Kettering Hospital the following week and privately John was dreading it. He felt so much happier in Ireland but he was steeling himself to make the trip because he knew he had to go through with it. On the drive back to Dublin that Sunday afternoon he tried to put it out of his mind and concentrate on the evening that lay ahead. Bill Durkan had arranged a family dinner at Jurys Hotel, Carol and her parents would be there and the idea was that they should all enjoy themselves before John and his wife prepared to go back to New York.

John, walking from the car park to the hotel, suddenly lost his balance. The others helped him to his feet and most of them put it down to weakness caused by the illness. His mother was not so sure. Beatrice Durkan could tell that her son was not himself during the meal. She knew the return to America was preying on his mind and she detected the same build-up of anxiety that she had seen before the blackout in September.

When they returned home, John went straight to bed. Danny, his eldest brother who was working with his father in the building business and was mostly in London, went into John's room and the pair talked until the early hours. Not long after Danny eventually went to bed, Aidan Durkan was woken by some sort of sixth sense and seconds later he heard a dull thud in the bathroom. He got up to see what it was. He was shocked to find John lying on the floor. He called Danny and his parents. Between them they carried John to his room and put him back into bed. Bill Durkan rang for an ambulance and John was rushed to St James's Hospital. He arrived shortly before 4.00 am and promptly had a blackout.

Five hours later he was still in a coma and the doctors told the family that they did not expect him to regain consciousness. 'If he does, will he be paralysed,' asked a distraught Beatrice. 'Will he be able to speak?' The doctor shrugged his shoulders and said he did not know. It was the first time that Beatrice had completely given up hope. Until that moment, her son's belief in his ability to recover had persuaded her that he would make it. There had, of course, been many times when she had doubts. But she had only to speak to her son for the hope to come flooding back. When John had returned from America the previous month, she had seen how much happier he was and she felt that being in Ireland was the tonic he needed. She would see him in the sitting-room happily watching the racing on television and marvel at how he was able to put his illness to one side.

Carol sat with him on the bed in St James's. She too had been told by the doctors that this was almost certainly the end and she was determined to stay with her husband until the last. Shortly after 5.00 pm, with the lights in the streets outside revealing the beginning of the evening rush hour, John sat up. There was a big smile on his face, almost as if nothing had happened. Carol could hardly believe it and nor could Beatrice. They both felt it was a miracle.

He was kept in hospital for several days, but the return to Sloan Kettering was cancelled. However, the coma had left its mark; he seemed to be drained of what little energy he had before it happened and again his condition deteriorated. He was anxious to spend Christmas at home, his parents were keen to have him with them and eventually the doctors decided that it would be safe for him to do so. Istabraq was due to run at the big Leopardstown meeting, but unlike the previous year, there was no question of John going to see him run. He was far too ill for that.

A number of people called to see him including JP McManus and Ed Byrne, the photographer who had taken some of the pictures for the brochure that had been intended to help launch John's training career. But Byrne was suffering from a cold and he dared not stay longer than ten minutes in case John caught it.

The AIB Agri-Business December Festival Hurdle was on the Monday, the last day of the four-day meeting, and this time Aidan O'Brien took the precaution of running a pacemaker. Iacchus had won on his hurdling début at humble Tramore over sixteen months earlier, but he had not been successful in any of his thirteen subsequent outings. Indeed, on his most recent appearance, he had finished last. He was ridden by Colm Murphy, a capable amateur who worked as racing secretary at O'Brien's Piltown yard and he started at 150–1. Punting Pete, who had run twice since Tipperary, was again in the field, as was Gazalani who had been beaten twenty-three lengths into fourth in the Hatton's Grace. The only other runner was Lady Daisy who was not without a chance on the handicap ratings. She was on 139, 16lb behind Istabraq and she received 12lb. She started second favourite at 11–2 and Istabraq was completely unbackable at 1–6.

Punting Pete did the pacemaker's work for him and Iacchus, who finished tailed off, could never get closer than second. Charlie Swan rode Istabraq as he was to many times afterwards, particularly at Leopardstown, as if it was impossible for him to get beaten. He sat as still as a statue almost throughout and let out an inch of rein in the straight to allow his mount to dispute the lead with Punting Pete approaching the last. But he did not pass Punting Pete until he had jumped the final flight. He continued to sit motionless as the favourite strode away to win with any amount in hand.

Sadly for John Durkan, the race was not shown by RTE which traditionally covers only the first three days of the meeting; three days later – on New Year's Day – he had to go back into St James's Hospital. He had seen his home for the final time and he went down hill rapidly. 'The last few weeks were awful,' remembers Carol. 'He was in a lot of agony and the doctors could not do much for him by this stage.'

Some of his friends continued to ring and Eddie Hales, for one, was struck how in the final few days of his life, when he knew he was dying, JD's first thoughts continued to be for others. He shrugged aside questions about his own well-being to ask how Jamie Osborne's hand was progressing. Osborne had severely damaged his hand and his wrist when Space Trucker unseated him on the horse's chasing début at Cheltenham in mid-November. Durkan was concerned that the man who he had known so well in Lambourn and who had taken the trouble to fly to America to see him, would miss Cheltenham.

Bill Durkan had already begun to think about the funeral. He had been to many others in his life and he had often felt that so much of the money spent on flowers was wasted. He did not want to see thousands of pounds worth swept away into black rubbish bags after his son's funeral, not when the money could be put to much better use. He wanted it to go to leukaemia research. He believed that if only the specialists could identify the gene that caused the disease, they would be able to find a cure for it. He decided that he would set up the John Durkan Leukaemia Trust Fund to raise money for a special unit at St James's Hospital.

On the night of Wednesday, 21 January, John Durkan died. He was only thirty-one. Even though his death had been coming for a long time, it left the Hyde and Durkan families with a terrible sense of loss. His parents were deeply affected and so was his brother Aidan who was once again blaming himself, albeit unfairly, for falling ill on the day before the transplant. He was still convinced that if the doctors had been able to use his bone marrow, John's body would not have rejected it and he would still be alive. But the grief was hardest of all to bear for his widow. The man she loved was no more and he had suffered so terribly in his final few months, particularly in the last three weeks.

On the Thursday arrangements were made to inform the newspapers and to get the funeral in motion. The death notices asked for no flowers to be sent, other than those from the immediate family. Instead, donations could be made to the leukaemia fund. The papers, particularly the *Racing Post* and *The Sporting Life* (which was less than four months away from closure), called on many of those who had known Durkan well to pay tribute. Ferdy Murphy, who had worked for the family in the days of Anaglogs Daughter and who had done much of the training, put into words what many had only dared think by saying: 'When somebody like John goes in this way, you sometimes wonder whether there is a God up there.'

Murphy, who now trains in Yorkshire, recalled the racing-mad teenager: 'He would come home from school, drop his school bags and rush out into the yard. There was a daily battle with his mother who wanted him to do his homework. It didn't matter what I asked him to do, even the dirtiest of jobs. As long as it was with horses, he would do it. He was an absolutely cracking kid. He was tremendous fun to be with and he managed to live life to the full without ever upsetting anybody. It is so sad to lose him.'

Paddy Prendergast, the Curragh trainer for whom John had ridden winners, said: 'He was a great horseman and a very good rider, but most of all he was a gentleman.'

The tributes came even from beyond the racing world and Niall Quinn, the tall Sunderland and Irish international footballer, struck a chord with many when he said: 'I've known his family since I first came to England many years ago. He always made me feel very welcome and I remember his car screeching to a halt early one morning in Newmarket when I was walking to the newspaper shop. I didn't know whether to think it was a mugger or what, but it was John. He picked me up, collected the newspapers and gave me a guided tour of John Gosden's stable. He just couldn't do enough for people. I am at a real loss to describe how I feel, and I was very empty when I heard the news.'

The removal of his remains to St Patrick's Church in Glencullen near the Durkan family home took place at 5.00 pm on the Friday and the funeral was held at 11.00 am on the following day. There were so many mourners that the service had to be broadcast by public address system to all those who found the church already packed to capacity by the time they arrived. On the specially printed service sheet was written: 'His merry spirit seems our comrade yet, free from the power of weariness and pain, forbidding us to mourn or to forget.' Jamie Osborne, tears in his eyes and emotion in his voice, gave the address:

> Over the last sixteen months, we have all prayed that today
> would never be upon us. JD fought harder than we will ever
> know to try to prevent it. His strength and hope shone through
> the last months of his life, leaving us bewildered at his
> determination. Everyone here will feel the same when I say that
> my life has been enriched through my friendship with John. He
> was a truly remarkable man and a wonderful friend. He was
> our standard setter. The shocking brevity of his life means that
> his friends have many years left to cherish his memory.
> The world is full of terrible events but to us gathered here
> today, this is the worst. Hope and happiness are strangers
> standing way over the horizon, apparently impossible to reach.
> But it will not always be like this and around the flame of his
> memory we will one day be able to lift our hands and feel the
> warmth of his character with us still.

John Durkan was buried in the cemetery next door to the church. Afterwards his father invited the mourners to join him at a gathering in Dublin's Burlington Hotel. At the race-meeting at Thurles that afternoon, racegoers stood for a minute's silence in JD's memory. They did the same at Leopardstown the following day when Istabraq ran in the AIG Europe Champion Hurdle.

Istabraq had only six opponents, all trained in Ireland. The race was worth £50,000, but no English trainer saw much point in going to the trouble and expense of sending a horse over just to get trounced by a potential champion. Old rivals Punting Pete and Cockney Lad were in the line-up and so too, interestingly, was Noble Thyne who had beaten Istabraq on his hurdling début at Punchestown fourteen months earlier. But this was his first race for nearly six months and the Paddy Mullins-trained eight-year-old started almost unbacked at 25–1. Mullins, just back from a holiday in Morocco, also saddled Notcomplainingbut, although she too was little fancied.

A more potent threat was expected to come from His Song who had notched up three wins in novice company in impressive style. Novices had run well in the AIG in the past – Danoli had finished second in 1994, and three years before that Nordic Surprise had won as a four-year-old. Favourites, though, had a surprisingly poor record and only two had been successful since the famous Dawn Run fourteen years earlier. Two of those beaten favourites, Morley Street in 1992 and Halkopous twelve months later, had started at odds-on. Indeed, four of the seven most recent previous winners had started at 10–1 or more. There were also niggling doubts about the health of the O'Brien horses, which were not firing with their customary all-guns-blazing devastation. The stable had had only one winner from thirty-five runners since the beginning of the year. Admittedly thirteen had been placed, but even they included three beaten favourites. Yet Istabraq was strong in the market and the book-makers were forced to cut their opening 2–5 to the slightly shorter 4–11.

O'Brien also ran Theatreworld. The previous year's Champion Hurdle runner-up had been switched to the Flat during the summer and had done well, winning three of his five starts. However, he had been disappointing in his three subsequent runs over hurdles. He had started odds-on for the Lismullen Hurdle at Navan in November and been slammed nine lengths by Cockney Lad, and he had run far worse when a remote fifth to the same horse at the County Meath course shortly before Christmas. In The Ladbroke he had finished with only two behind him and was reported to have made an ominous choking noise. However, Norman Williamson was asked to fly over from England to ride him, underlying how seriously O'Brien viewed this race for the horse, but punters were unimpressed and Theatreworld was allowed to drift, almost unbacked, from 12–1 to 20–1.

Charlie Swan, wearing a black armband as a personal tribute to the man who had been buried the previous day, settled Istabraq in mid-division as Punting Pete, ridden by Richard Dunwoody, set off in front. Those who had backed the favourite were given some heart-stopping moments, because Istabraq did not jump with his usual fluency. The crowd gasped in horror as he hit the fourth hurdle, and with his judgement seemingly affected, he went into the next all wrong and hit it hard. Swan sat tight, for he had known that the mistake was coming. 'We got our wires crossed,' he said. 'Istabraq was a bit long at the hurdle and I asked him to take off, but I only half-asked him. He went to jump, changed his mind and tried to put in an extra stride.'

Istabraq was soon back on the bridle and jumping much better. By the time they reached the second last he was cruising, whereas the others were being ridden along. Richard Hughes, thrilled to get the chance of another ride in a big jump race, drove His Song into the lead early in the straight. Swan gave his mount a squeeze and Istabraq was alongside. The champion looked across at Hughes, driving His Song for all he was worth and savoured the sight.

Not until he had jumped the last did he say go. He gave Istabraq three backhanders in quick succession and the favourite accelerated clear to beat His Song by a length and a half. Noble Thyne was three lengths back third and the rest were strung out with the washing.

Bill Durkan was among those who welcomed Istabraq into the winner's enclosure. So too was Carol Hyde who had been in two minds about whether to go to the meeting. The previous three days had been more traumatic and emotionally draining than almost any in the last fifteen months, and the easy option would have been to stay away. She decided, however, that she owed it to her husband to go and watch the horse who had meant so much to him. When JP McManus quietly asked her to accept the trophy from Taoiseach Bertie Ahern on his behalf, she happily accepted. She thought it a touching gesture.

A few weeks later McManus made another. Because he was so busy with his business in Switzerland, he needed somebody to liaise with his various trainers and send him reports about all his horses. He thought Carol, with her knowledge and her background as well as her conscientious approach to life, would be ideal for the job. Again she was delighted to accept: 'When John died, I thought that my whole world had fallen apart, but the job has really helped me. It has kept me busy and kept me going. I find the work very interesting and I love it.'

Istabraq's AIG performance was seen by most observers purely as a chance to assess his prospects of winning the Champion Hurdle, and again the initial judgements were given by the representatives of the big bookmakers, who like to put any changes in a horse's Cheltenham price in front of the television commentator within seconds of the winner passing the post. Several layers were singularly unimpressed and lengthened Istabraq's price – Dato Star had beaten the 1996 Champion Hurdle winner Collier Bay by twenty lengths in his first race of the season at Haydock the previous day and he looked a viable alternative. David Hood, the former jump jockey who represents William Hill, was among those who felt Istabraq had been unconvincing.

'Not too many SunAlliance Hurdle winners have got quicker with age and I think the two miles of the Champion Hurdle is Istabraq's bare minimum,' he said. 'Unless the ground at Cheltenham is bottomless and it seldom is, Istabraq is going to be susceptible to a horse with a little bit of toe.' Aidan O'Brien though, saw things differently and he knew there were solid grounds for believing that the horse would prove to be a far better animal by the time Cheltenham came round:

> The pace in the AIG had been a bit messy, despite Punting Pete going off in front, and Istabraq had raced too keenly. This was why he had not jumped particularly well. Charlie told me afterwards that he was idling and not concentrating properly. But I would rather he made mistakes in a race like that than at Cheltenham. The previous season his jumping there was better than it had been in his races in Ireland, because he needs a strong pace to bring out the best in him. Apart from getting him ready for his first outing of the season at Tipperary, we had planned to only really train him for one race, the Champion Hurdle. Istabraq had developed and become stronger by the time of the AIG. The time to start serious training was after it. He came back from the race with a nick in his stifle, but it was very minor and it did not hold us up.

The man who rode Istabraq at home was Pat Lillis. The son of a County Limerick farmer who kept the occasional point-to-pointer on his land at Athea, Lillis started in racing at the apprentice school in Kildare. He worked for Dermot Weld for nearly two years before increasing weight persuaded him to switch to jumping stables. He moved back to County Limerick to join PP (Pat) Hogan, a brilliant trainer of point-to-pointers and hunter chases but a notoriously hard taskmaster, before going to England to work for Jenny Pitman. His race-riding ambitions were largely unfulfilled. He had had one ride in a bumper by this stage and a few more in point-to-points, but none of his mounts had won.

Young men like Lillis tend to move on once they realise they are not going to get rides, and from Mrs Pitman he went to Newmarket to John Gosden. After a year at Stanley House, he planned to move again, this time to John Durkan. He was twenty-five when he followed Istabraq to Ballydoyle and two months later he became the horse's regular rider. Few others at the yard have ridden the horse since, and as Istabraq is exercised seven days a week, Lillis has been kept busy. 'He did have two weeks off at one stage,' said Aidan O'Brien, grinning broadly. 'He got married and we sent him straight off to the Breeders' Cup. He had to wait until he got back to have his honeymoon.'

It is a little ironic that Lillis, a man who failed even to get off the ground floor as a jockey, should have become one of the star work riders at the famous stable. Istabraq is just one of several big name horses that he rides in their work and he rates Istabraq with the best of them:

> Over a trip, say a mile and a half to two miles, he would be as fast as any of the top Flat horses we have had. In his first season he would take a strong hold but as the years have gone by, he has become more switched off and he is now a straightforward ride. His routine does not change much. He pulls out at 7.30 am, and he is on the gallops by 8.00 am. He does a warm-up canter over a couple of furlongs and then a good swinger down the back over a mile and a furlong. Theatreworld usually leads him and we normally work in single file. I don't think I have ever backed him and I have never ridden him schooling. Aidan won't let me.

The work at Ballydoyle effectively takes place behind closed doors. There is an uphill gallop, built early in 1999, visible from the Cashel/Clonmel road that goes past the front gates, electronically operated by a security guard, but the main gallops are completely out of sight. However, the big British bookmakers have a highly sensitive grapevine – often triggered by an unusual amount of money for one of the other horses in a big race – and this invariably picks up the slightest setback to a leading fancy. In the second week in February, some of them believed that all might not be well with the Champion Hurdle favourite and they marked him out in the betting. One bookmaker reported support for Grimes, a 20–1 shot who was trained by Christy Roche but owned by McManus. The obvious inference was that Grimes might deputise if something had happened to Istabraq. For once though, the rumour mill had it wrong. 'They were just rumours, nothing more,' said O'Brien. 'There was never anything wrong with Istabraq in the build-up to that Champion Hurdle.'

Theatreworld was also to run in the big race. He had finished second last in the AIG but at Navan seventeen days later he upset the odds laid on Cockney Lad. O'Brien ran him again ten days afterwards and he beat Noble Thyne in the Red Mills Trial Hurdle at Gowran Park. But he made hard work of it and he hardly looked like a horse who had finished second in a Champion Hurdle. His trainer thought differently: 'Theatreworld is a gross, heavy horse who takes a lot of work to get him fully fit. People have often said that he has a wind problem, but he hasn't. With him, it's a bit like asking a fat man to run two miles. You would think he had a wind problem by the time he got to the finish! Theatreworld was getting fitter with every race and we knew that come Cheltenham, he would be ready to run another big one.'

9 Ista Business

Istabraq was now being trained in earnest and Tommy Murphy, despite all his years of experience, was amazed at the amount of work the horse was asked to put in. 'In the last three weeks before the Champion Hurdle, Aidan really tightened the screw,' he said. 'All the horse's work continued to be with others leading him and it continued to be on the bridle – in all the time Istabraq has been here, I have never seen him off the bit at home – but he was made to work faster and faster. The horse stood up to it well. He is really tough and he has a great heart, but there was a fair bit of mileage on him by the time he got to Cheltenham.'

Murphy is good for his age – he was sixty-three when Istabraq won his third Champion Hurdle – and he still has a full head of hair, albeit grey. He comes from Kilmore Quay in County Wexford and he served his apprenticeship with Milo Walshe at Kilmacthomas in County Waterford. He was seventeen when he rode his first winner at Pheonix Park in 1953, but he had to wait until he was thirty-two for his first major success, Pianissimo in the 1969 Phoenix Stakes. He was then riding for Clem Magnier at Athboy in County Meath and lived nearby. He also rode over hurdles, twice winning the Galway Hurdle and in 1972 partnering Noble Life to victory in the Gloucester Hurdle (now the Supreme Novices). He rode for many years for Vincent O'Brien. He had his best season in 1978 when he was champion jockey with sixty-six winners on the Flat. The previous year he won two classics for O'Brien, the Irish 1000 Guineas on Lady Capulet and the Irish St Leger on Transworld. The big-name horses that he rode to victory included Storm Bird, Be My Guest, Solinus and Godswalk.

He continued riding until he was forty-five, when he took a job as assistant trainer to Mick O'Toole on the Curragh. After one season there and a further three as assistant to Frank Dunne at Dunboyne, he moved to Ballydoyle to join David O'Brien. When the latter gave up training two years afterwards, Murphy crossed the gallops to join Vincent O'Brien. On his retirement, Murphy became assistant to the new incumbent. His specific responsibilities include the bandaging of Istabraq's fore legs. Anita Harvey is the only other person entrusted with this and it is usually Murphy who does it:

> First thing every morning I go down to Margo's Yard and put new bandages on. Istabraq is such a good mover that he stretches right out and comes back on his pasterns. This wears down the heels. His feet are also vulnerable because he has four white hooves, but the floating chip never seems to bother him. Normally I don't have to put a head collar on when I am doing the bandaging. He stands still and lets me work away, but in the last ten days before Cheltenham he is quite different and he is always on the move. He is primed up and becomes edgy and a bit anxious. Mind you, Aidan gets a bit edgy come Cheltenham time too!

Early in the weekend before the Champion Hurdle, Charlie Swan drove to Ballydoyle to ride out Istabraq and pop him over a hurdle. He was delighted and a little surprised to find the horse better than he had ever known him. He said as much to the trainer. 'He will bloody destroy them,' replied O'Brien. Swan, who had seldom heard O'Brien use any sort of swear word, was struck by the force with which the words had been delivered. 'But Aidan,' he said. 'this is the Champion Hurdle.' The reply was unhesitating. 'I don't care. He will destroy them.'

Swan was far from convinced: 'While I had always felt Istabraq was a serious horse, I had doubts about him over two miles. I tried to pretend that I didn't and in various interviews with the press and on television, I said I thought he had enough pace to win the Champion Hurdle. Privately though, I thought that two and a half miles was his trip. JP was confident it was two miles and Christy Roche also thought he had enough pace for the Champion. I reckon I was the biggest doubter of them all and while I kept my thoughts to myself, I made up my mind to jump him out smartly rather than ride him for speed.'

Istabraq travelled with Theatreworld from Shannon on the day before the meeting, with Pat Keating in charge. The travelling head lad comes from Athy where his father is a mechanic. He has no family connection with racing, but he joined Willie Bourke's small stable when he left school. He switched from Bourke in the County Wicklow village of Grangecon, made famous by Francis Flood and the legendary Paddy Sleator, to Victor Bowens who trained only a few miles up the road, and used the 'railway' gallop on which Sleator trained so many of his big race winners. Like Clifford and Lillis, Keating had few race-riding opportunities. He is much taller and heavier than the other two and his only rides were in point-to-points. He moved south to Mickey Browne at Cashel and a job with Vincent O'Brien was a logical progression. He was eighteen when he went to Ballydoyle in 1985, a year that stands out in his memory as the one in which Law Society won the Irish Derby. He no longer rides out but whenever he is not away racing, he gives the rest of the staff a hand with mucking out the boxes and with whatever else needs to be done.

Istabraq went into the race with nine successive victories behind him, but other statistics were not quite so favourable. No Irish-trained horse had won the Champion Hurdle since Dawn Run fourteen years earlier and the field of eighteen was the biggest since Granville Again won in 1993. The main dangers appeared to be Dato Star, who had not raced since his devastating victory at Haydock in January, and I'm Supposin. This six-year-old, ridden by Swan to finish fourth to Make A Stand twelve months earlier, was now the mount of Richard Dunwoody and had left the opposition for dead in his most recent start, beating Master Beveled by nineteen lengths in the Axminster Kingwell Hurdle at Wincanton. He and Dato Star shared second favouritism at 6–1. The bookmakers opened Istabraq at 9–4 and when they found that there was no great flood of money for the horse, they lengthened his price to 3–1. McManus decided this was value and stepped in to put on £30,000 with Victor Chandler, one of the few brave enough to stand such big bets.

Theatreworld started at 20–1, and Aidan O'Brien had already backed him. O'Brien has never been much interested in betting, but the previous year he had offered his staff a £500 bet on the horse of their choice. They had opted for Theatreworld, each way at 33–1. When O'Brien offered them the same bet again this time, they had little hesitation in going for the same horse and they got on early at 40–1.

Fortunately for Victor Chandler, O'Brien had gone to another bookmaker. St Patrick's Day had all the makings of a St Valentine's Day massacre for the bold-laying Chandler, who had his worst-ever Supreme Novices Hurdle result when French Ballerina powered home seven lengths clear of His Song at 10–1, costing him well over £100,000. His liabilities on Istabraq were £150,000 even before JP stepped in, and he lost again when the heavily backed Unsinkable Boxer won the final race of the afternoon. The Irish had a setback in the second race when

Hill Society was beaten a short head in the Arkle Trophy – Dunwoody reckoned he was in front just before the line and again just after it. Noel Meade, Hill Society's luckless trainer, had been trying for twenty years to have a winner at the Cheltenham festival and he was to have to wait another two before he finally achieved it. Little wonder that when he did, he knelt down and kissed the hallowed turf in the winner's enclosure as if he was the Pope arriving in Poland.

Istabraq knew where he was and what was coming long before he was led into the paddock. But once there with the crowds and the noise all round him, the memories came flooding back with a vengeance. Unable to control his nerves any longer, he broke into a sweat. By the time Charlie Swan took him out on to the course, there was a white lather on the horse's neck. However, unlike twelve months earlier, Swan did not worry about this. Aidan O'Brien had told him how he had watched the videos of some of the great horses trained by Vincent O'Brien and how many of them sweated up quite considerably before their big races. Swan also believed that the sweating was taking the pressure off him. 'I felt I had a ready-made excuse if I got beaten,' he said. 'When they sweat up like that, you can always blame the horse!'

Swan's wife Tina, watching proceedings from a box in the stands, was nothing like as calm as her husband. She knew that the race meant an awful lot to Charlie because it was his ambition to win one of the three biggest races in the jumping calendar – the Grand National, the Cheltenham Gold Cup and the Champion Hurdle – and she is normally so worried that her husband will get hurt that she stays at home. The stress of ambition and risk of injury was too much for her to bear. In even more of a sweat than Istabraq, she turned her back on both the view from the course and the television in the box. Whenever anyone told her how the race was progressing, she replied that she did not want to hear a word until it was over.

Jason Titley, successful on Royal Athlete in the 1995 Grand National, set off in front on Lady Daisy, a 100–1 chance trained by Tony Mullins who had the misfortune to be jocked off Dawn Run when she won the Champion Hurdle and again when she won the Cheltenham Gold Cup. But the pace, Swan was convinced, was nothing like fast enough. He needed it to be a real test of stamina: 'I wanted a lead but I was almost tempted to make it.' He drove Istabraq determinedly into the fifth hurdle: 'I'd studied it when I walked the course beforehand. It's a vital hurdle, you meet it going uphill and if you miss it, you can lose the race. I saw a lovely stride as we approached it and I kicked him into it to make sure he winged it.'

Titley had no such luck with Lady Daisy, who made a mistake and dropped back as Dunwoody swept into the lead on I'm Supposin. Swan sat still until he reached the top of the hill and then he started to niggle. At the third last Istabraq jumped past I'm Supposin, and still worried about the trip, Swan headed for home:

> I had to make it a test of stamina. I was under the impression that the others were queuing up behind me, waiting to challenge. Not until I saw the rerun did I realise that they were all off the bridle at this point. But I could hardly believe how well Istabraq was travelling. When he jumped the second last, he picked up again and he was really running rounding the final turn. So often in big races, I say to myself coming to the last 'I just hope he meets this one right,' but Istabraq was spot on and he really pinged it. Sixty yards after the final flight, I looked to my right. I couldn't believe I was so far in front. But the crowds were making such a noise that I felt there had to be something coming. I didn't want to go on hitting the horse if I was well clear, so I looked again, this time to the left. There was nothing there.

Theatreworld, just as he had done twelve months earlier, galloped relentlessly up the hill to deprive I'm Supposin of second place, and rewarded the staff at Ballydoyle with the place part of their free bet. Fourth was the Martin Pipe-trained Pridwell who had lost valuable ground at the start, a factor that was to have a significant bearing in calculations, or rather under-calculations, two and a half weeks later. Last of the fifteen finishers was Lady Daisy and one place in front of her was Grimes, the horse who had been backed when the rumours about Istabraq's health had spread so erroneously the previous month. Poor Shadow Leader fared even worse. The previous year's Supreme Novices winner fell heavily at the last and broke his neck.

The twelve-length winning margin was the biggest since Insurance had won by the same distance sixty-six years earlier. In that race there were only three runners and it had still to achieve real status; even the County Hurdle carried more prize money in those days. Istabraq's time was good – less than a second slower than the course record set by Make A Stand a year earlier.

Carol Hyde, watching the race from the McManus box, was near to tears: 'It was an unbelievable feeling when Istabraq passed the post in front,' she said. 'I would have loved it if John had been there to see it and I think everybody was thinking of him that day.' Many were. Bill and Beatrice Durkan went into the winner's enclosure and so did some of their children. *Sky News* asked Carol to do an interview about her husband but shy and saddened, she declined. Her father spoke instead.

So did McManus who, when quizzed by the press, said: 'The whole day has been very, very special for me, my family and John Durkan's family. I would never have been fortunate enough to own Istabraq but for John. Thinking about him makes us realise how lucky we are to be coming to Cheltenham. Winning is a bonus.'

McManus, who admitted that he had hardly dared watch the closing stages of the race, refused to disclose how much he had taken out of the ring. He smiled and said it was enough to pay for a good party. He invited forty people to join him for dinner at the Lygon Arms that evening and even though the Broadway hotel is not cheap, the £90,000 he won would have paid for many such parties there!

The following day's *Racing Post* carried an advertisement from Sheikh Hamdan's Shadwell Stud, congratulating O'Brien and McManus. It was headed 'Istabraq ista business.' In *The Sporting Life* was one from Ladbrokes stating: 'Roofer required. Apply Cheltenham Racecourse.'

Two evenings later, on a much more sombre note, a memorial service for John Durkan was held in Lambourn's small Catholic church where he used to pray when he was living at Ashdown. There had been a similar service at Newmarket the previous Sunday.

Istabraq lost remarkably little weight in the course of his visit to Cheltenham and when Aidan O'Brien put him on the scales on his return to Ballydoyle, he was pleasantly surprised to discover that the horse was only between four and five kilos lighter than when he left. He had lost more weight in his races in Ireland that season and O'Brien had little hesitation in deciding to fly him to Liverpool for the Martell Aintree Hurdle on Grand National day.

There were widespread fears that terrorist threats would again disrupt the fixture and on the Friday, the middle day of the meeting, an alarm went off in the County Stand; it had to be evacuated and racing was temporarily suspended. That same day police in Ireland found 1000 pounds of explosives in a car at Dun Laoghaire. It was believed that the car was to be driven to Aintree and blown up the following day. Rain proved to be almost as big a threat and one which the intense security presence had no power to prevent. It poured down on Friday night and it continued on Saturday. The official going – soft, heavy in places – was altered to heavy for the Martell Aintree Hurdle.

O'Brien and McManus debated whether to withdraw Istabraq, but the owner felt that he should take his chance. 'When you are actually there at the racecourse, I always find it hard to take a horse out,' he said, 'and we made the decision to run.'

There were only six runners and all bar Collier Bay had run in the Champion Hurdle. The 1996 champion had not raced since his eclipse by Dato Star at Haydock in January, but there were some unusually bullish noises emanating from his stable. Jim Old, a normally reserved trainer, was quoted in that day's *Racing Post* as saying: 'I would have preferred another week with Collier Bay, but I think I've got him pretty close to his best. If I've done my job properly, he will run very well. I certainly wouldn't be surprised if he won. I don't think the Champion was a great race – Istabraq didn't beat Pridwell any further than we did in 1996. People have got carried away with the manner of the victory, rather than with what Istabraq actually beat.'

Collier Bay was marginally preferred in the market to Pridwell, who had been forced to make up for his slow start at Cheltenham by travelling round the whole field to get into a challenging position at the top of the hill. He had been beaten just over fourteen lengths, half of which was accounted for by his poor start and at least five lengths by having to go wide.

Istabraq's price eased from 4–9 to 4–6 and it was at about this point that his owner struck. McManus was reluctant to recall how much he had on, but it was a lot: 'I thought he was a very generous price and I decided to back him.' One bookmaker accepted a bet of £130,000 to win £80,000. It was, at the time, one of the biggest bets ever recorded on a racecourse in Britain and there was only one man who could have placed it. It was hardly surprising that Istabraq's price shortened to 4–7.

Carl Llewellyn, who was to win the Grand National an hour later, made the early running on Kerawi, but only reluctantly, and Charlie Swan was far from happy about the pace he set. Mick Fitzgerald on Collier Bay took over at the fourth, but the pace was still only modest. At the fourth from home, Tony McCoy took it up on Pridwell (Collier Bay was a spent force and he had to be pulled up before the second last), but it soon looked as if Swan had his measure. Swan's mud-spattered face had that by now familiar grin of triumph spread across it as Istabraq jumped the last upsides Pridwell, but it was soon wiped off as Pridwell responded gallantly to McCoy's determined driving. Approaching the line Pridwell got his head in front and Istabraq was beaten for the first time since his hurdling début at Punchestown nearly seventeen months earlier. Even today, Swan blames himself:

> When we jumped off, nobody wanted to make it and we went no gallop. I should have dropped him out stone last and got him relaxed. But I had him a little bit handier than I should have done and he ran a bit keen. He wasn't used to going so slowly in a race and he guessed at a few of his hurdles. He also let fly at the odd one. I then had him racing a bit early,

Tommy Murphy wins
the 1980 National
Stakes on the brilliant
Storm Bird in the
colours of Robert
Sangster.

Going down to the start
for the 1998 Champion
Hurdle. Note the sweat
on Istabraq's neck.

The 1998 Smurfit Champion Hurdle. Richard Dunwoody leads on I'm Supposin. Istabraq is on the left and the injury-prone Dato Star on the heels of the leader.

Clear at the last. Charlie Swan's triumphant grin says it all.

Istabraq strides up the hill twelve lengths clear. The horse in dark colours following him home is Theatreworld, finishing second for the second time.

This is only number one. Charlie Swan indicates that there is more to come.

Heading towards the last in the Martell Aintree Hurdle and Istabraq is closing on Pridwell.

Hail the conquering hero. The worried-looking man beside Charlie Swan's left elbow is Cheltenham managing director Edward Gillespie.

Istabraq's highly
effective hurdling
technique is shown in
this picture at Cork in
November 1998.

The final flight in the Martell Aintree Hurdle.
Swan's triumphant grin did not last long.

Ferdy Murphy, an
eloquent Yorkshire-
based Irishman with a
roller-coaster career.

Charlie Swan laughs as
the French Holly bubble
is burst in the 1999 AIG.

Going down to the start for the 1999 Champion Hurdle and Istabraq is awash with sweat. Looking on anxiously are (left to right) Anne Marie O'Brien, Tommy Murphy, Irish course commentator Des Scahill and Aidan O'Brien.

Istabraq's second Champion Hurdle in the bag. Theatreworld becomes the first horse to finish second in three successive Champion Hurdles. Third (on the right) is French Holly.

Noreen McManus holds the Smurfit Champion Hurdle trophy aloft. Michael Smurfit looks on.

Joyous scenes in the winner's enclosure as Charlie Swan attempts a Frankie Dettori. In the foreground, second left, is Bill Durkan.

Shell Champion Hurdle. Note how far Istabraq
stands off at his hurdles.

Enda Bolger, returning
on Risk Of Thunder,
prepares to hurl Charlie
Swan's whip into the
crowd.

Both arms broken.
Charlie Swan displays
the end result of Hot
Bunny's Roscommon
fall. Note the mobile
phone lead plugged into
his ear.

Defeat at Fairyhouse. Limestone Lad (Shane McGovern) lowers the champion's colours. Charlie Swan was criticised for giving Istabraq too much to do.

The Bowe family can hardly believe it. Michael Bowe, who does all the training, is next to the horse's head.

Istabraq first....the rest nowhere. The finish of the 1999 December Festival Hurdle. The winning margin was officially fifteen lengths but it looks a lot more.

Easy in the AIG. Stage Affair (Tony McCoy) chases Istabraq home. Limestone Lad (almost obscured by the runner-up) ran way below his best.

'Riding this horse is like driving a Rolls Royce,' Charlie Swan tells Aidan O'Brien. Davy Clifford and Pat Keating are with the horse. Looking on are Timmy Hyde and Carol.

Mobbed by the media. Istabraq is surrounded by the press as he returns to the AIG winner's enclosure.

The final flight in the 2000 Champion Hurdle.
Istabraq sweeps past Blue Royal (Mick Fitzgerald).

V for Victory. Charlie
Swan acknowledges the
cheers of the crowd.

Istabraq joins the immortals as he returns to the
winner's enclosure. Edward Gillespie is a worried
man once more.

Up Ya Boya. Brendan
Grace bursts into song.

The 2000 summer holiday was spent at Ballydoyle.
Darapour follows Istabraq round the field.

Immortal....How the
Racing Post reported on
a moment of racing
history.

A picture of contentment.

and I had to get him settled again. After running that bit keen, he got tired in the closing stages. The really heavy ground that day had nothing to do with it. I would never blame the ground with Istabraq. He goes on any going and he handles soft, even heavy, better than most horses. For some reason though, he does tend to jump a bit better when it's faster.

McManus was saddened by the defeat, not because of the money he lost – he took that with good grace – but because the champion's colours had been lowered. 'I always regret it when a good horse gets beaten,' he said, but O'Brien was philosophical. 'They all get beaten eventually, most of them anyway. In any case the ground was very bad and Charlie didn't abuse him. I think he was minding him, because of the ground.'

The stewards expressed no such sentiments about Pridwell's rider and they suspended him for four days for using his whip with excessive force. 'McCoy hit Pridwell seven times from the last hurdle and six of them were very hard,' said William Nunneley, one of the stewards' secretaries. The RSPCA was moved to speak out and Bernard Donigan, its equine consultant, said that Istabraq would have won if McCoy had not transgressed the whip rules. But Swan did not agree, saying: 'Tony was harder on Pridwell than I was on Istabraq because his mount was responding. I felt Istabraq was giving me all he had to give. If I had been harder on him, it would have made no difference to the result.'

While Istabraq was enjoying his summer holiday out at grass at Martinstown, his trainer and his jockey were reorganising their lives. Aidan O'Brien's string of Flat horses at Ballydoyle was increasing in number and quality. Four weeks after Istabraq's defeat in the Martell Aintree Hurdle, O'Brien won the 2000 Guineas at Newmarket with the aptly named King Of Kings. Less than five weeks later he won his second British classic, the Oaks with Shahtoush. He also had other high-class three-year-olds in Second Empire and Saratoga Springs.

Even though he has a prodigious appetite for work, it seemed pointless to go on making the fifty-mile round trip to Piltown each day and devoting so much of his time to horses who were usually racing for comparatively little reward. There was also the danger of burn-out. O'Brien decided that he would train solely at Ballydoyle and confine himself to the Flat, apart from the small number of jumpers stabled in Margo's Yard. Frances Crowley, Anne Marie's sister and the fourth eldest of Joe Crowley's six daughters, was keen to start training. Her father owned the land and gallops at Piltown, so it was the obvious place for Frances to train.

She had already proved herself. In the 1994/5 season she became the first of her sex to be Ireland's champion amateur, and the following season she shared the title with Willie Mullins. She then turned professional and she had ridden seventy-one winners by the time she took out a trainer's licence for the start of the 1998/9 season. She was twenty-five. Not all the owners stayed with her, but there were enough horses for her to run eighty-five over jumps in her first season and for her to finish fifth in the table. She was also winning races on the Flat.

O'Brien was still only twenty-eight when he gave up the reins at Piltown and effectively kissed goodbye to his domination of Irish jump racing. He had been champion trainer in every one of the five seasons he had held a licence and he had also been the leading trainer in terms of numbers of winners each time. He had averaged 119 winners a season – the record before he eclipsed it, had stood at seventy-eight.

At the beginning of July 1998, Charlie Swan started training. He took over his father's licence at Modreeny, built a barn to accommodate more horses and set about moving the whole operation up a gear. Not long afterwards he announced that he would no longer ride in steeplechases. 'My nerve over fences was not as good as it had been and as a result my love of riding in chases was not as strong,' he admitted. 'There was also the possibility of injury. If you are riding a horse as good as Istabraq, you don't want to risk getting broken up by riding any old thing over fences.'

Swan had dominated the Irish jumping scene almost as completely as O'Brien. He had been champion for nine consecutive seasons – a remarkable achievement in an occupation fraught with danger. In the 1992/3 campaign, he became the first to ride over 100 winners and he repeated the performance in three of the next five seasons, most notably in 1995/6 when he rode 150 winners. At Listowel on 22 September 1997 he became the first Irish-based jump jockey to ride 1000 winners. These included fifty-nine on the Flat. At Haydock on 2 May 1998 he became the first to ride 1000 winners over jumps when winning the Crowther Homes Swinton Handicap Hurdle on Rainbow Frontier, the horse on whom he had achieved the previous landmark over seven months earlier. However, the decision to start training, closely followed by the one to confine himself to riding over hurdles, indicated that his brilliant riding career was drawing to a close. Swan admitted as much, but he was reluctant to think of a time limit. 'I still enjoy riding over hurdles, even though I am not as hungry for success,' he said. 'I don't get the same kick out of winning small races down the country and I possibly ride more tactically than I used to. I've tried to get wiser as I have grown older. Having Istabraq to ride was a big part of my decision not to retire.'

10 Murphy's Law

Istabraq's first race of the season was again the John James McManus Memorial Hurdle, but this time the course at Tipperary was unable to stand up to the rain and the Saturday fixture had to be postponed to the following Thursday. The course was still waterlogged at this stage and so the meeting was transferred to Cork three days later.

When Mallow racecourse was renamed Cork during 1996, the level of the racing surface was raised by between two and three feet in a bid to stop the track being so susceptible to flooding. The problem was that the River Blackwater which runs alongside the course had a tendency to burst its banks. During the winter months the course was often flooded for days, even weeks on end and the problems were accentuated by the water taking a long time to find its way back when the river fell to more normal levels. Half a dozen huge culverts were installed in the car parks as well as on the course to drain the floodwater back into the river. The culverts were fitted with non-returnable sluice valves to stop the river flooding back in again.

John Harvey, the clerk of the course, was adamant that the culverts and sluices were so effective that racing could take place forty-eight hours after any flooding. The snag on this occasion was that the flooding occurred on the night before the meeting. Tentative arrangements were made to postpone it from the Sunday to the following Tuesday. At 2.00 pm on Sunday four pumps were switched on and the staff began work. They continued all through the night and by halfway through Monday morning almost all the water had drained away. The one exception was at the far end of the sprint course, and so it was decided to run the fixture without the five furlong nursery.

The most intriguing of Istabraq's five opponents was Master Beveled, who had beaten the ill-fated Shadow Leader in the Agfa Hurdle at Sandown in February, and who was trained near Welshpool by former jump jockey David Evans. There is an old adage in racing that you should never be afraid of one horse, implying that it is always worth taking on a supposed good thing if your horse is the next best, the reasoning being that something might go wrong with the favourite. Even so, Evans' assertion that 'You never know what might happen if Istabraq has an off-day' had a supremely optimistic ring to it. Master Beveled was only fourth favourite.

Lady Daisy, second favourite at 7–1, made the running until Charlie Swan allowed Istabraq to go clear after jumping the second last and, despite a slight mistake at the fourth flight, the 2–7 shot won every bit as effortlessly as his price suggested he should. Master Beveled to some extent vindicated his trainer's opinion by finishing second and collecting over £11,000, to encourage the Welshman to return.

'When I schooled Istabraq at Ballydoyle before the original Tipperary date, he gave me the impression that he had become stronger since the previous season and the race confirmed this,' said Swan. 'He ran a bit keen in the early stages but when he met the fourth wrong he quickly corrected himself.'

Aidan O'Brien was at Louisville in Kentucky preparing Second Empire for a tilt at the Breeders' Cup Mile at Churchill Downs four days later. He was in contact with his wife at Tipperary via her mobile, both before and after the race, although not during it. 'I didn't want to listen in to the commentary because I had become a bit nervous about the outcome,' he said. 'It was Istabraq's first run of the season and things had not gone according to plan, with all the postponements and the transfer of the race from one course to another.'

There were no such worries with the Avonmore Waterford Hatton's Grace Hurdle at Fairyhouse just under four weeks later and Istabraq started at 5–1 on to take his hurdles tally to twelve from fourteen starts. Only Nomadic, third in the previous season's Triumph Hurdle and more recently conqueror of Commanche Court in the Morgiana Hurdle at Punchestown, was thought to have any chance – and so it proved.

Istabraq took off a fraction too soon at the fourth flight and kicked the top bar out of the hurdle, but otherwise it was a flawless performance. He went to the front at the third last and strolled home with Charlie Swan almost contemptuously allowing Nomadic to get within half a length at the line. Master Beveled was six lengths back third, this time rewarding Evans with only £3600.

At Newcastle the previous day, Dato Star had run out an impressive five-length winner of the Fighting Fifth Hurdle to emphasise his

Champion Hurdle claims. But this gelding, trained at Norton in North Yorkshire by Malcolm Jefferson, had had a succession of injuries and setbacks. Early in 1997 he was found to have suffered a strain to his off-fore suspensory ligament, and in the following year's Champion Hurdle he skinned a hind leg. He did not race again until the Chester Cup in May, when he was pulled up before halfway in a state of near collapse, and was discovered to have a fibrillating heart. He was hardly reliable material for an ante-post bet on a race as demanding as the Champion Hurdle, yet the Newcastle win saw his Cheltenham price tumble from 25–1 to 12–1. Istabraq was hot favourite at 7–4 and French Holly, the horse who was beaten by Dato Star in the Fighting Fifth, was pushed out to as much as 20–1.

All that was to change before the year was out because the big, powerful French Holly put himself into the forefront of the hurdling picture by demolishing the opposition in the Pertemps Christmas Hurdle at Kempton. He beat Master Beveled by nine lengths, with Dato Star another eight lengths back – this time the horse finished lame. The runner-up had been receiving 5lb when beaten six and a half lengths into third in the Hatton's Grace and, given that Istabraq had won so easily at Fairyhouse, French Holly's performance was still some way below that of the reigning champion. But it was enough to promote him to second favourite in the Champion Hurdle lists.

The manner of French Holly's win also overshadowed Istabraq's second successive December Festival Hurdle victory at Leopardstown the following day. Only two horses took on Istabraq, neither had a hope on form and the champion, starting at 10–1 on, treated them with the expected disdain. Ferdy Murphy promptly announced that French Holly would take on Istabraq in the AIG Europe Champion Hurdle just under four weeks later.

Murphy, an eloquent Yorkshire-based Irishman, had had a roller-coaster career both before and after his stint with Bill Durkan. The son of a tillage farmer in Aidan O'Brien's home town of Clonroche, he had already had considerable hunting and show-jumping experience by the time he joined Vincent O'Brien's brother Phonsie at the age of sixteen. But his plans to become a top jockey looked liked evaporating when he managed only five winners in his first seven years. He thought a move to Danny Kinane (uncle of Flat champion Mick Kinane) would put him on the right road, but he stayed at the Mullinahone yard for only a season before deciding to quit racing. 'I was having serious weight problems and finding it harder and harder to diet. I moved to London to work on the building sites,' he said. 'The work was so hard that I lost two stone. When I was down to 9st 7lb, I felt I should give racing another go and I returned to Ireland to join Paddy Mullins.'

Five years as a jockey and two years as the Goresbridge trainer's head lad followed before he left racing again, this time to run a pool-table and slot-machine business in Donegal. But the government effectively drove him back into racing by outlawing the machines, and Murphy moved to Dublin to work for Durkan. The problem was that although Murphy did most of the training, Durkan held the licence and the limelight. Trainers need to get their names into the papers if they are to attract patronage. Murphy was still riding in races but beset by difficulties with his weight once more; he was unable to do less than 11st and his 100-plus winner career was already past its peak when he partnered Anaglogs Daughter to win the 1980 Aynsley China Cup Chase at Chepstow.

'I kept going but I was struggling and one day at Naas, clerk of the scales Percy Banahan caught me cheating trying to do 12st 5lb – I had deliberately left the girths behind when I went to weigh in. He gave me a right bollocking and I thought "Sod this – I'm only kidding myself".' '

The ex-jockey with training ambitions moved to Woodbridge in Suffolk to act as private trainer to Geoff Hubbard but, as with Durkan, it was Hubbard who held the licence and Murphy's part in the stable's success story went unheralded. It was only his boss's increasingly poor health that brought Murphy recognition. 'In 1991 Mr Hubbard wanted to spend quite a lot of time out of the country and under Jockey Club rules he was not allowed to do that as well as hold the licence, so it was transferred into my name. I was meeting people at the races every day who said that if I ever wanted to become a public trainer, they would send horses to me.'

'In 1994 I decided to do just that and I rented a yard in Somerset. I calculated that I would have thirty horses, but I ended up with only twelve – and I struggled once more. At least I did until I found good owners like Paddy O'Donnell and Kieran Flood (owner of French Holly), and after a bit the yard was not big enough for all the horses. Robert Ogden asked me to train for him but he said that he would not have anything in the south of England. I moved north, found a yard in Middleham and Ogden bought it. But soon we were not getting on, he took the horses away and asked me to vacate the yard.'

Yet again Murphy was struggling but he managed to find a place with eighteen boxes five miles away, and close to the celebrated High Moor gallop. At the 1996 Cheltenham festival he sent out two winners, Stop The Waller in the Kim Muir and Paddy's Return in the Triumph Hurdle. He was well and truly on the map and at the time of the AIG he had over sixty horses.

The previous March French Holly had won the SunAlliance Hurdle by fourteen lengths and put up a performance that Timeform considered to be the equal of any in that novice race since it first brought out its

Chasers & Hurdlers annual in 1976. But French Holly's victory had come when Istabraq's twelve-length Champion Hurdle win was fresh in Murphy's mind. 'It was less than twenty-four hours after Istabraq had destroyed the opposition and my initial reaction was that there was no point in ever taking him on,' he said. 'I told the press we would aim French Holly at the Stayers' Hurdle the following season, but I also said to Kieran Flood that we should meet at my yard in three months' time, pool our ideas and decide our plans. When we met, Kieran pointed out that French Holly would almost certainly be the only chance he would ever have of winning a Champion Hurdle. Paddy Mullins had always taught me never to be afraid of any one horse on any one day, and so we mapped out a campaign that would take us towards the Champion. We included the AIG knowing that we would have to take on Istabraq, but I didn't see that as a bad thing.'

Unfortunately for Murphy, he had reckoned without the unpredictable nature of the weather in the middle of winter. He had thought he had planned for all contingencies when deciding to fly French Holly to Ireland; this was much more expensive than going by sea, but at least there was no risk of delay caused by high winds. French Holly left his box in North Yorkshire before first light on the Friday, two days before the race and was driven to the East Midlands airport. But when he arrived the fog was starting to come down. Several hours later, when there was no sign of it lifting, the flight was cancelled. There was no guarantee that the situation would be any better the following day, and so Murphy elected to send the horse by sea. French Holly was driven across the country to Holyhead for the three-and-a-half-hour ferry journey to Dun Laoghaire. He finally arrived at Leopardstown on Saturday morning, having been in the horsebox for over twenty-four hours. It was hardly the ideal preparation for taking on the best hurdler in the world.

There was no outward sign that French Holly's long journey had taken its toll when he arrived, and nor was there the following day. However, had he been a human athlete, it would surely have left him feeling some way below his best. It is hard to believe that his bid was not doomed to failure even before he reached the start.

However, the Istabraq camp, hearing only third-hand reports that the challenger's journey to Ireland had not been an easy one, were treating French Holly with caution and respect. 'I was there when he won the SunAlliance so easily,' said O'Brien. 'He was obviously a very good horse and we were worried about him.'

'I didn't know quite what to expect,' said Swan. 'I couldn't really see that he was going to beat us – I thought Istabraq would have too many gears for him, but I'm always a bit afraid when there is so much hype about a horse. There seemed to be an awful lot of confidence behind French Holly.'

He started 9–4 second favourite, and he was the only one of the four challengers to be seriously considered, even though the quartet included the useful David Nicholson-trained Zafarabad. Adrian Maguire set off in front on French Holly at a searching gallop, particularly considering how heavy the going was, and Swan was content to sit some six to eight lengths behind him. But after the leader had made a mistake at the third last, Istabraq began to reduce the leeway. Approaching the last he was level, with Swan's only movement being to turn his head to the left to give the hard-at-work Maguire a long and seemingly disdainful look. He did it again after jumping the final flight and deliberately did not let his mount draw more than a length clear. It was a display of confidence, almost cockiness in which Swan clearly revelled and he and Istabraq returned to thunderous applause from the big crowd.

'Charlie gave Istabraq a great ride that day – he kept him on the bridle and really saved him,' said O'Brien. 'And I was a bit surprised how easily we beat French Holly.' So was Swan: 'Adrian set a right gallop and it was not until the second last that I really knew I was going to win. French Holly suddenly seemed to be in a bit of trouble and at the same moment Istabraq came alive in my hands.'

Murphy was determined to try again in the Champion Hurdle – he was convinced that the long journey had taken a terrible toll on his horse and he said as much at a Cheltenham preview in Cork in early March. It was at the same venue as the one in which Aidan O'Brien had been subjected to persistent questioning about the riding of Finnegan's Hollow two years earlier. One member of the audience said that if what Murphy had told them was correct, why had he not withdrawn the horse? The AIG was surely a waste of time and effort? 'It wasn't,' replied Murphy. 'The owner went home with ten grand in his arse pocket!'

Early in February Cheltenham racecourse, as part of its publicity drive for the festival, obtained O'Brien's permission for a group of British racing journalists to see Istabraq at Ballydoyle. O'Brien caused more than a few raised eyebrows and several column inches of print, by remarking that Istabraq had become so fast in his home work that he wondered whether he would get the trip in the Champion Hurdle. It was a curious thing to say about a horse who had proved he stayed two miles and five furlongs when winning the 1997 SunAlliance Hurdle; horses tend to lose speed as they get older, particularly on the Flat, but they do not lose stamina. Timeform took the Ballydoyle trainer to task in its 1998/99 *Chasers & Hurdlers* annual, saying: 'What must he have been thinking about?'

'It was really only a passing remark,' O'Brien explained. 'Istabraq had done himself very well after the AIG and he weighed about 510 kilos when the English press came to Ballydoyle that morning. He had become very rounded, almost like a sprinter, and very quick in his work. I therefore said that I wondered if he would get home up the hill at Cheltenham – and he was still about 510 kilos when he left for the Champion Hurdle.' Racing journalists were not the only ones to visit Istabraq that month. JP McManus called to see his famous horse and he walked down the long drive to Margo's Yard with the trainer, only to peer over the door of the box and find Istabraq fast asleep. 'We'd better not disturb him, we'll come back later,' said O'Brien, leaving McManus to marvel at the sympathy and understanding shown towards the horse.

'I feel very privileged to own a horse as good as Istabraq,' he said. 'He is a big part of my life and of my family's life too. He determines where we all are and even when we go on holiday. But I don't think it is fully appreciated just what a wonderful job Aidan has done with him. Although it may not be obvious to somebody not closely involved with the horse, Istabraq is very highly strung. People often say that it is easy to train a good horse, but I don't think that applies to this one. Aidan's attitude, when he saw him fast asleep that day, really brought home to me just how skilful his approach is with Istabraq.'

McManus had even more reason than usual to look forward to Cheltenham because he looked like having major contenders in several of the races. Earlier in the season he had bought the top French four-year-old hurdler Le Coudray and after a twenty-length defeat of Limestone Lad at Naas, the gelding looked certain to be one of the favourites for the Stayers' Hurdle; in the Supreme Novices he had Joe Mac and Cardinal Hill; Darapour and Khayrawani were to go for the Coral Cup; Spot Thedifference the National Hunt Chase and Youlneverwalkalone the Champion Bumper. The last-named met with a setback, but all the others made the meeting to give McManus the strongest team of any owner.

However, he got off to a bad start. Joe Mac was beaten seventeen lengths by Hors La Loi III in the opener, and Cardinal Hill was already under pressure when he unseated his rider at the second last. There was no question of attempting to recoup his losses on Istabraq. He considered the price of 9–4 on too short to risk having a bet and statistically it was hard to disagree with him. Istabraq was the shortest-priced favourite in the Champion Hurdle since Sir Ken had won the third of his three Champion Hurdles at the same prohibitive odds in 1954. The bookmakers, who had been expecting McManus to strike, were surprised to find that the biggest recorded bet was one of £50,000 to win £25,000. French Holly drifted from 9–2 to 11–2 as many believed that the going, officially good to soft and soft in places, would not be testing enough to bring his undoubted stamina to the fore. It was 16–1 bar the first two and Theatreworld, again carrying the £250 each way bet given by O'Brien to his staff, started at this price.

Once more Istabraq suffered from Cheltenham nerves and he sweated up before the start. But Swan already had French Holly in his sights when Andrew Thornton kicked for home on the second favourite after the third last. Istabraq jumped past French Holly at the next and he was six lengths in front by the time he reached the last. He maintained that advantage over Ferdy Murphy's hope all the way to the line, with the Tommy Treacy-ridden Theatreworld plugging on bravely to divide the two, and become the first horse in history to finish second in three successive Champion Hurdles.

Istabraq was the third Irish-trained horse to retain his Champion Hurdle crown, following Hatton's Grace and Monksfield, but it was not a performance of the same brilliance as a year earlier, and the time was over two seconds slower than that recorded by Hors La Loi III in the Supreme Novices. Swan was inclined to blame the going and, perhaps a little unfairly, himself. 'Istabraq did not show much in the way of acceleration because the ground was a little bit dead. If it had been good, he would have quickened much better,' he said. 'At the second last I had gone long on him, but he was clever enough to put down and put in a short one. He met the last all wrong and I let him pop it. On that sort of ground, I probably went for home a bit too early.'

11 Injuries and Defeat

The Punchestown festival the following month had been increased to four days for the first time and the feature race on the final day was the £110,000 Shell Champion Hurdle. It had been put on specifically to attract Istabraq, and there was therefore no need for the horse to return to Aintree. O'Brien and McManus, however, were keen to avenge that defeat by Pridwell and they decided to run Istabraq in both the Martell Aintree Hurdle and the Shell Champion.

It was an ambitious plan. Inside seven weeks Istabraq would be asked to take on the best the opposition could muster in three championship races, he would have to make four flights and contend with two pre-race overnight stays in strange stables. It would be an ordeal for most horses and it could well test Istabraq's delicate mental make-up to the limit. The Martell Aintree Hurdle had proved the undoing of several Champion Hurdlers even before Istabraq met his Waterloo in the 1998 race. The two races are very different – Aintree is three and a half furlongs longer and is run on a sharp track whereas Cheltenham is a testing course, particularly on the final uphill climb to the winning post. See You Then, three times winner of the Champion Hurdle, had been unable to win the Aintree race and more recently Granville Again, Flakey Dove and Make A Stand had all been beaten in it after winning the Champion. Sometimes the reason had been lack of stamina, in other cases the horses had been unable to repeat the brilliance they had shown at Cheltenham because the race came so soon afterwards.

All but one of Istabraq's six opponents had run at Cheltenham, the exception being Stretarez who had never raced over hurdles. Not surprisingly, he was hardly considered in the betting and the only one who was thought capable of springing an upset was again French Holly. 'He had improved since Cheltenham and I questioned whether Istabraq really stayed two and a half miles,' said Murphy.

Istabraq started at 2–1 on and McManus backed him. 'I thought the price was generous enough,' he said, but his punt was modest by his standards and the biggest recorded bet was £20,000 to win £10,000. Tony McCoy set a blistering pace on Deano's Beeno, and when the seven-year-old faltered, Richard Johnson on Midnight Legend took over at much the same searching gallop. Charlie Swan was convinced that they were both out to kill off Istabraq's finishing kick.

> The ground was pretty quick at Aintree that day, one of the fastest he had ever raced on. He seemed to handle it well, but they went a right gallop. I felt they were trying to do Istabraq for stamina. Deano's Beeno was soon flat to the boards and so were one or two of the others. I was just about the only one on the bridle and I thought they must be going too fast. I decided to take a chance, drop my horse right out and take my time with him. Fortunately, I read it right and he arrived to win his race full of running.

Swan waited until after he had jumped the last before heading French Holly, and much as he had done in the AIG in January, Istabraq cruised home to win hard held by a length. Sadly, the inexperienced Stretarez paid a heavy penalty. He fractured a cannon-bone just before the final flight and he had to be put down. National Hunt racing is an exciting sport that fires the emotions and in Ireland most racegoers much prefer it to the Flat, which is seen as clinical and almost cold by comparison, but it can exact a cruel toll on its participants. French Holly was killed seven months after the Martell Aintree Hurdle; he fell and broke his neck on the schooling grounds on High Moor. At the beginning of 1999 Noble Thyne, the horse who had beaten Istabraq on his jumping début at Punchestown in November 1996, had to be put down after breaking a hind leg in a beginners' chase at Fairyhouse. On the second day of the 1999 Punchestown festival, Joe Mac collapsed and died after being pulled up at the end of the Stanley Cooker Champion Novice Hurdle; a post-mortem revealed a massive internal haemorrhage.

The jumping game can also kill those who ride the horses and Paul Carberry, who had partnered Bobbyjo to victory in the Grand National less than an hour after the Martell Aintree Hurdle, nearly died of an internal haemorrhage. Ten days after the National, he had a fall riding work on Noel Meade's sand gallop and one of the horses behind fell over him, kicking him in the back and fracturing a rib. Preliminary X-rays revealed nothing more serious than the rib injury, but over the next three days Carberry felt worse and worse. He drove to Camas Park to spend Friday night there. The next morning he was in such agony that he thought he was going to pass out; only afterwards did he discover that it was because oxygen was not getting to his brain. Carol Hyde insisted on calling the family doctor who had him rushed to Cashel Hospital in an ambulance. The doctors at the hospital diagnosed a rup-tured spleen and carried out an immediate operation. They found three litres of blood spilling around his stomach. If it had not been for Carol's insistence, he would have died that day.

Carberry was still in hospital when the Shell Champion Hurdle was run. Somewhat understandably, none of those Istabraq had beaten at Aintree took him on and nor did any of those who had finished behind him at Cheltenham. The principal opposition was provided by the English-trained pair Sir Talbot and Decoupage (first and second in the County Hurdle), the Grand Annual Chase winner Space Trucker and the progressive Limestone Lad who had won his last three starts.

Tony McCoy tried to make the most of Limestone Lad's proven stamina, and he set out to stretch the field, but he never succeeded in causing Swan a moment's anxiety. Istabraq moved smoothly into the lead early in the straight and ran out an effortless winner from Decoupage, with Limestone Lad five lengths back third. This was Istabraq's seventeenth victory from his nineteen outings over hurdles and many of the 20,000 racegoers rushed to see him return to the winner's enclosure. They cheered Swan to the echo when he celebrated his triumph by firing his whip into the crowd.

Only Swan was aware of the irony of the gesture. The previous day Enda Bolger, going out for the final ride of his career on Risk Of Thunder in the La Touche Chase, had asked Swan if he could borrow his whip for the occasion. Bolger had ridden a world-record 412 point-to-point winners and the La Touche (Ireland's longest race, with thirty-one obstacles including banks and stone walls) was his 120th success on the racecourse. As he rode into the winner's enclosure to tumultuous cheers, he picked up the whip he had borrowed and hurled it like a spear into the sea of faces on the far side of the enclosure. Its owner, who had watched in horror as the whip disappeared into the six-deep ranks of spectators, rushed round to try and retrieve it. When he eventually tracked down the souvenir hunter, he had to do a bit of explaining before he could recover his property. Afterwards Swan felt that he had not acted with the decorum expected of a champion and he decided that if he won on Istabraq, he would return the whip to the crowd.

Charlie Swan had one of the worst falls of his long career at

Roscommon at the beginning of August. The course is shaped like an oblong with the corners rounded, but they still make for sharp bends which some horses have difficulty in negotiating. Swan was riding Hot Bunny in the Sallymount Maiden Hurdle and as it was the first three-year-old hurdle race of the season, none of the eleven runners had any public jumping experience. Swan was moving the filly into a challenging position after the fourth last when the accident happened:

> The ground was a bit quick but there was still some dew on the grass. Hot Bunny leaned in towards the rails as she went round the bend at the end of the back straight. She lost her front legs and fell. I put out an arm to save myself and I was kicked on the other arm by one of the horses behind. Both arms felt sore and dead and I was hoping that that was the extent of the damage. After a couple of minutes I knew they were broken and I thought 'Oh no. Not this again'. My next thoughts were 'How long will I be out of action? Will I be back for Istabraq at Tipperary?'

Swan has a long history of broken arms. The first break came on his first ride at Cheltenham on Irish Dream in the 1987 Triumph Hurdle. She swerved to try to avoid a faller at the last, Swan put out his left arm in a bid to break the fall and he heard the bone snap as he hit the ground. He was champion for the first time when Chamois Boy fell with him at the 1990 Galway festival and slammed his hoof down so hard on the jockey's right arm, between the elbow and the wrist, that the arm was broken in two. Swan, in terrible agony, could hardly believe it when he saw that only the skin was holding the two halves together. In October 1991 he broke a bone in his right hand and just over two years later he broke one in his left hand. In December 1995 he broke his right arm below the elbow (again as a result of putting it out to save himself) in a fall in a novice chase at Clonmel. The break was in a piece of bone that had been broken in the Chamois Boy fall. Swan did not give it enough time to heal and he eventually had to have an operation and a plate inserted. There are two scars seven inches in length on his right arm, the result of this and the Chamois Boy plates. On his left arm is a similar scar, left by the operation to insert a plate after the Irish Dream fall.

Fred Kenny, the surgeon who carried out all the operations, had warned Swan that his arms would not withstand too many more breaks; they would soon reach the stage where they would refuse to mend and as the arms were set in plaster in Roscommon Hospital that evening, this preyed on Swan's mind.

Some weeks later, when the time for him to resume race-riding neared, Swan was also concerned that it could affect his nerve. It is not only bones that refuse to mend. The thought of falling from a horse at over 30 mph and being kicked and trampled on by the horses behind, each weighing half a ton and delivering blows with metal-tipped hooves with the force of a pile-driver, is terrifying. It forces some jockeys to give up the game early in their careers. For others, the adrenalin-surging excitement of riding winners fills their minds to the exclusion of any thoughts of fear. But each break, and more particularly each spell on the sidelines, gives the mind more encouragement to dwell on the dangers and for many their nerve eventually cracks. They are forced to give up the game and find a less dangerous way of earning a living. Swan was thirty-one, he had been riding over jumps for fourteen years and he was uncomfortably aware that the clock was ticking away. He returned to the fray at Gowran Park ten days before Istabraq's first run of the season and he was pleasantly surprised.

'I thought I would be a bit nervous and that the fall might have affected my nerve,' he said. 'When I come back from injury, I am always a little worried that I am going to fall or get kicked on the bone I have broken. But once I was on the horse, I felt fine. My nerve had not been affected at all.'

He had to wait for Istabraq for a winner. David Evans again sent over Master Beveled for the John James McManus Memorial Hurdle and for the third year in a row the heavens opened. The going was officially soft to heavy but was variously described by the jockeys as very deep, bottomless and even unraceable. But it made not the slightest difference to Istabraq who moved smoothly up to the pace-setting Limestone Lad between the last two flights and swept clear to win effortlessly. Limestone Lad was beaten seven lengths with Master Beveled eight lengths away in third.

Limestone Lad was beaten by McManus's Le Coudray at Navan next time, but a week later he won by nine lengths at Naas. The following week he easily won the Morgiana Hurdle at Punchestown and his connections decided to take on Istabraq in the Hatton's Grace Hurdle. The seven-year-old was fast acquiring cult status. Punters love a horse that keeps winning and Limestone Lad had won seven times so far that year. What made him all the more special in the eyes of the public was that he was owned and trained by a hitherto unknown country farmer who had been trying all his life to come up with a good horse.

James Bowe farms 200 acres at Gathabawn near Johnstown in County Kilkenny. He started training point-to-pointers in 1950 and he used to ride them himself. He won six races as well as two bumpers. He also bred the 1981 Queen Mother Champion Chase winner Drumgora. He was in his seventies when Limestone Lad came along, and early in

1999, when Limestone Lad was beaten twenty lengths by Le Coudray at Naas, he had his audience roaring with laughter when he claimed that his horse would have won but for missing three days work because he himself had been away at cattle marts. But the way the horse kept winning, repeatedly defying the handicapper's attempts to anchor him, led many to believe that Bowe might have been right.

All the training of Limestone Lad was done by Bowe's eldest son Michael who had had some modest success as an amateur, including two bumpers on Le Pearl in 1981 and two races over hurdles in 1983. He also rode Limestone Lad in a bumper on one occasion, but he vowed never again after finding him difficult to manage. However, he continued to ride the horse in all his exercise and work at home. As Limestone Lad was the only racehorse the Bowes had – they usually sold most of the ones they bred – he was always exercised on his own. He went out seven days a week, even on Christmas Day and Michael and his father discovered that the more the horse raced, the better he became.

They tried various jockeys, but the one they felt suited the horse best was the little-known Shane McGovern. From Beauparc near Navan where his father makes pub furniture, he was twenty-two when he rode in the Hatton's Grace and he had ridden the same number of winners. Significantly, he had won on all his four rides on Limestone Lad. He started in racing when he was fourteen but he had to wait four years for his first winner and he was still claiming a 5lb allowance in November 1999. Because of the value of the race, he was unable to claim in the Hatton's Grace and the Bowes held a family conference before deciding that he should keep the ride.

David Evans sent over Master Beveled yet again, but only Limestone Lad merited any consideration by the punters. He started at 13–2 with Istabraq 7–1 on. Limestone Lad had won most of his races by going off at a blistering pace and galloping the opposition into the ground. He would obviously attempt to do so again, but there was some doubt about whether his inexperienced rider would be able to judge the pace correctly, and considerable doubt as to whether it would be fast enough to fluster Istabraq.

Swan was not unduly concerned and said: 'While I have a healthy respect for Limestone Lad, I don't see any reason why he should beat me. Istabraq obviously won't be 100 per cent fit at this stage of the season, but he will be fit enough to win. I will probably settle him in second or third, because I would not want to let a horse as good as Limestone Lad get too far in front.'

McGovern had been given his instructions when he rang Michael Bowe the previous evening. 'The better the start you get, the better the race will go for you,' he was told. 'Pop him out and let him gallop, let him be himself and do what he wants. He is as well as he has ever been.'

The young rider thought he was going to steal a march when the jockeys were called in and Limestone Lad was right against the tape whereas Istabraq was almost sideways on. He was disappointed when the starter changed his mind, and ordered the jockeys to turn their mounts and come in towards the tape a second time. But McGovern still got the start he wanted.

'Limestone Lad was jumping out of his skin. It was unbelievable how well Mr Bowe had the horse,' he said. 'I knew I was a good way in front when I couldn't hear any hurdles clattering behind me. I didn't feel as if I was going that fast, but I wasn't sure because he has such a long stride that it makes you think you're only going a handy pace. I didn't look back.'

Swan's immediate thought was that his rival had blown it. 'I was going fast enough even though I was soon twenty lengths or so behind the leader. I thought he wouldn't be able to keep it up,' he said, before revealing that his feeling of confidence was short-lived. 'As we went past the stands for the first time, I began to pray that Limestone Lad would come back to me. By the time we got to Ballyhack (the highest point on the course) he was even further in front and at this stage I knew I was in big trouble – unless he completely capsized. Just before the turn into the straight Limestone Lad seemed to falter for a few strides and I thought I was going to catch him. As we ran down to the last, I again thought I would beat him. I got to within two lengths, possibly less, when he picked up again. The ground was pretty heavy and Istabraq was tired. I was disappointed we got beaten, but I don't think I was as disappointed as everybody else seemed to be.'

Swan was referring to the crowd and the critics in the press room. Some of the British-based ones picked up their pens in earnest and lambasted Istabraq's rider for giving the champion too much to do. Swan did not agree:

> Aidan O'Brien had said to me before the race 'He is going to get beat one of these days,' and afterwards he told me not to worry about it. He said he would prefer to see the horse getting beaten and coming back in one piece, than having a very hard race. If the Hatton's Grace was run all over again, I wouldn't ride it much differently. Istabraq gets two and a half miles alright but I thought he looked big beforehand, and he probably wasn't fully fit. It's early in the season when your main race is the Champion Hurdle. The way Limestone Lad has developed he will always be very hard to beat over that trip, particularly given the gallop he can go.

Swan had his point rammed home for him at Navan thirteen days later when he rode Le Coudray in a two and a half mile conditions race. This time McGovern was able to claim his 5lb allowance and his mount dished out to Le Coudray the same punishing treatment he had given Istabraq, before drawing right away to win by twenty lengths. There was a possibility of the Bowes deciding to take on Istabraq again in the December Festival Hurdle, but by now they were entertaining thoughts of the Stayers' Hurdle at Cheltenham, and they decided to run instead in the three mile Christmas Hurdle on the previous day.

Limestone Lad had only four opponents, he started at 6–1 on and he set off at his usual furious pace. The other four riders – Charlie Swan, Paul Carberry, Conor O'Dwyer and Pat Malone – made no attempt to give chase and some spectators jeered as they passed the stands with a circuit to run. By the time they got to the fifth hurdle, Limestone Lad was a furlong in front. With half a mile to run, all four were riding hard but they were all beaten a distance or more. They were hauled before the stewards who took a poor view of their riding. 'We felt they made no effort to keep in touch with Limestone Lad and it looked terrible,' said Peter Matthews, the senior stewards' secretary. The stewards fined the four jockeys £250 each and ordered them to forfeit their riding fees. They were informed that they had breached rule 212 which deals with non-triers. They regarded this as the ultimate insult. 'Even Istabraq would have had trouble going that gallop,' said a furious Swan. 'There will be no runners in this type of race if the stewards are going to do this sort of thing.'

The 'Leopardstown four,' as they briefly became known, had their sentences quashed on appeal. The December Festival Hurdle was tame by comparison. On paper Istabraq's task was only marginally more difficult than it had been twelve months earlier and he sauntered home to win as he liked. There was a lot more spice about the following month's AIG Europe Champion Hurdle because Limestone Lad was to take on the champion again. Also in the field was the useful novice Stage Affair, and Knife Edge who would have finished second in the December Festival Hurdle but for sprawling at the last.

This time, however, everything was expected to be in Istabraq's favour. Limestone Lad was unlikely to be as effective over two miles, and the yielding going was not thought to be sufficiently testing to bring his stamina into play. He had also been forced to miss a planned outing at Navan because he had been suffering from a skin infection and Michael Bowe feared he might not be fully wound up.

He started at 9–2 and Istabraq at 2–9. The rest, seemingly, did not count and this time Swan was careful not to let Limestone Lad get away. His task was made easier by the challenger not setting quite such a searching pace as usual. Indeed, with Istabraq cruising and never more than seven lengths adrift, it looked as if the leader was going nothing like fast enough. He was a beaten horse early in the straight and afterwards he was found to have suffered an over-reach to his near fore.

At Haydock the previous day Dato Star had once again put himself into the Champion Hurdle picture by beating Relkeel seventeen lengths, but the bookmakers were convinced he would not beat Istabraq who was now 5–2 on to join the illustrious group who had won the race three years in a row.

Aidan O'Brien set about his now customary build-up to Cheltenham, each week stepping up the horse's work, but at the same time being careful to do nothing that would upset him:

> Istabraq has a lot of brilliance but there is a very fine line involved and we have to ensure we keep on the right side of the balance. If he is asked to do anything different from what he normally does, he doesn't like it and he is inclined to fret. He lives on the edge. If you were to shout at him in his stable, he would break into a sweat.
>
> He is a natural athlete and a very clean-winded horse who does not need a lot of work, but we ask him to go a bit faster as Cheltenham draws near. We have also to draw the line between keeping him right and spoiling him. If we did the latter we would have to correct him and obviously we would not want to do that, so we try not to let him get too high an opinion of himself. It's different, though, when he gets to the racecourse, particularly Cheltenham, where he gets on a high. The adrenalin flows through him and it seems to pump up his muscles. Some class horses do this and with Istabraq it gives him extra strength and improves his performance.

In order to avoid infection being brought into the stables, every horse in Margo's Yard returns to an isolation box after it has raced. The one exception is Istabraq. He goes back to his own stable and the rest move out for the night!

In the second week of February the Ballydoyle team were given an unpleasant shock. Davy Clifford and Anita Harvey spotted a crack developing in the heel of one of Istabraq's hind hooves. John Halley was called in to have a look at it. The problem was serious. If Istabraq's work was continued, the crack would almost certainly widen and the horse might well be forced to miss the Champion Hurdle. If he was rested until the crack healed, he would miss a week of work and possibly two. He would then have to go to the Champion Hurdle only three-parts ready.

Ken McLoughlin took off the shoe and studied the crack several times. Halley did so too, and eventually they decided to opt for a third course of action. It would be a gamble but with the Cheltenham clock ticking away, they decided that it was a risk worth taking. The farrier screwed the two sides together with a plate and then used a material called equilox to build up a patch over the crack. Once this set, he found the hoof was strong enough for him to nail on a normal shoe. Istabraq resumed work the following day and, much to everyone's relief, the heel stood up to it. The crack healed well before Cheltenham.

It was a very private drama. No word of it reached either the press or the ultra-sensitive bookmaker grapevine and normality had long since resumed when Charlie Swan drove to Ballydoyle early on the morning of the Sunday before Cheltenham. It was only a fleeting visit; he had a runner in the 2.30 pm race at Naas plus three rides and he had another eighty miles ahead of him:

> I was actually on the horse's back for about thirty seconds. I
> got a leg up into the saddle, popped him over a hurdle and got
> off again. It was just to get his eye in. Aidan didn't want to
> upset his routine more than absolutely necessary, and as Pat
> Lillis knows the horse to a tee, there was no point in putting me
> up for a piece of work when I might go a bit faster or a bit
> slower than usual and upset the horse.

12 Up Ya Boya

At 11.30 am on Champion Hurdle day, Charlie Swan's mobile rang. It was Aidan O'Brien ringing to tell him that the decision had be taken to run. Half-an-hour later it rang again. JP McManus, acutely aware of the intense pressure on everybody involved with the horse, wanted to try to lift the burden of expectation from the shoulders of the man who now had to bear the brunt of it.

'If he wins, he wins – if he doesn't, don't worry,' said the caller. 'Ride him with confidence and if it comes your way, it comes your way. Just don't knock him about. There is no pressure.'

Swan was surprised to receive the call, not because it was rare for McManus to ring him – it was not – but because Istabraq's owner seldom gave him any instructions. Swan thought about what had been said and about the blood that had been found on Istabraq's nostril. At least, if the horse got beaten, nobody would blame him. But he had to forget about the scare and its consequences if there really was something wrong. He must concentrate on riding a race and on the opposition he had to beat. He had no ride in the Supreme Novices Hurdle and he viewed the result with mixed feelings. Paul Carberry made almost all the running on Sausalito Bay finally to end Noel Meade's Cheltenham hoodoo. Swan was delighted, not least because he had ridden for the County Meath trainer for several seasons and had been narrowly beaten on Meade's Heist in the Champion Bumper seven years earlier. However, Youlneverwalkalone had been made hot favourite to get McManus off to a winning start and the horse was beaten into third. It was a bad omen.

The Arkle Challenge Trophy went by in a blur as Swan concentrated on what was to come. He walked out into the paddock and across to the large group surrounding Aidan O'Brien and McManus. Anne Marie, Aidan's wife, was there and so were JP's family – wife Noreen and their two sons John and Kieran, and his brothers Gerry, Mike and Eoin. Carol Hyde was there too and her father Timmy who had done the bidding at Newmarket back in 1996. John Magnier and his friend Dermot Desmond, the Dublin financier, were with the group as were former Limerick hurling stars Eamon Grimes, Joe McKenna and John McDonogh.

Swan, who had been expecting a few light-hearted remarks to ease his own tension, soon realised that they were all as strung up as he was. Hardly a word was spoken by any of them, as their eyes followed Istabraq round the ring. Only occasionally did their gaze switch to any of the other eleven runners. Three of them were Irish: Theatreworld was running in his fourth Champion Hurdle (again the Ballydoyle staff's £250 each way bet was on him), Stage Affair was quietly fancied, but there was little support for Balla Sola, despite his defeat of Theatreworld in the Red Mills Trial Hurdle at Gowran Park the previous month. The injury-prone Dato Star was the shortest-priced of the British-trained runners that included Make A Stand, who had run the opposition ragged in the 1997 Champion Hurdle, and Hors La Loi III who had swept home seventeen lengths clear of the ill-fated Joe Mac (named after Joe McKenna) in the 1999 Supreme Novices.

The huge crowd, having read all about the nose bleed in their morning papers, had eyes only for the favourite. Istabraq was beginning to show ominous signs of nerves. The lower part of his neck was damp with sweat. As Aidan O'Brien legged Swan into the saddle, he said: 'If he's not going well, don't be afraid to pull him up.'

Remarkably, given that Istabraq could well be suffering from something that would only show up when the race began in earnest, there were some huge bets on him. The biggest recorded was one of £150,000 to win £75,000 and there was another of £50,000 to win £20,000. McManus was responsible for neither; he knew that he was taking a big risk in running the horse. To back him as well would be the height of folly.

Swan, the uncertainty still at the back of his mind, was encouraged by the vibes he got when he cantered Istabraq down to the start. The horse gave every indication of being in tip-top form and the jockey told himself that it was vital he obliterate all thoughts to the contrary:

> I had to make myself ride a normal race. I knew that if I was
> thinking about the bleeding and he made a mistake, I would
> imagine that there was something wrong with him even if there
> wasn't. Richard Johnson on Make A Stand took it up after the

first and he went very fast. He had gone past me going down to
the start, the saddle was up the horse's neck and he was
running too free. I thought that he definitely wouldn't finish if
he tried to keep up such a fast gallop and I settled Istabraq in
the middle of the field.

I got a nice run for much of the way, except just before the top
of the hill when Philip Hide on Mr Percy came in on me a bit.
As we started to come down the hill Istabraq was running
a bit lazily, I shook the reins at him and he suddenly came alive.
Norman Williamson's horse Katarino and Mick Fitzgerald's
mount Blue Royal, were both in front of me but they had been
jumping to the right, so I felt sure I would have enough room to
pass them on their inner. As we swept down the hill, I finally
knew I was going to win. Istabraq was really travelling and we
got a dream run through.

Istabraq was still on the bridle as he swept up to Blue Royal at the last,
and from that point on the course commentary was drowned by the
roars of the crowd. Istabraq strode majestically up the hill to join the
immortals. Swan waved his gloved fingers in a victory salute and
Istabraq swept past the post, only the fifth horse in history to win three
Champion Hurdles and the first since Persian War to win at four
successive Cheltenham festivals. The only others to do so were Golden
Miller before the Second World War and Arkle, the greatest steeple-
chaser of all time.

For once Theatreworld failed to land the Ballydoyle bet. He finished
with only two behind him – Make A Stand was last of all – but most of
the other runners were forgotten as racegoers rushed towards Istabraq,
by now making his way up the horse-walk towards the winner's
enclosure. Hats were hurled into the air and the cheering reached a
crescendo as the horse was led into jump racing's hallowed
amphitheatre, with Edward Gillespie struggling in vain to prevent hordes
of well-wishers following him through.

Among those who made the winner's enclosure was Brendan Grace.
The bearded comedian is an Istabraq fan but when McManus heard a
few weeks earlier that he had written a song heralding a third Champion
Hurdle victory, his first reaction was one of horror. He felt it was
tempting fate and 'would put the kibosh on the whole thing', but he was
impressed when he heard the tape. When Grace congratulated him and
burst into the Istabraq song, McManus invited Grace to join him for the
presentation ceremony and give a rendition to the crowd. Grace, with
Aidan O'Brien obligingly holding the microphone, sang only a couple of
verses. This is the full text:

It all began in 96 with a dream and a lad named John
His eyes would zoom on Sheikh Maktoum and a gelding young
    and strong
He approached JP to explain that he had a champion for
    the track
Soon a deal was tied by Timmy Hyde, it's the story of Istabraq.

He's a star on the Flat but I'll soon change that, claimed
    John Durkan with a smile
He got on the line to Aidan O'Brien, and they headed to
    Ballydoyle
He said the words come down from Martinstown, and there'll be
    no turning back
I want full compliance for the Sun Alliance, it belongs to
    Istabraq.

You're in the lead with fire and glory, striding speed, out on
    your own
A gallant steed of song and story…Istabraq, Istabraq, we'll
    cheer you home.

Well he won by far like a superstar and the field is running still
The cheer of the crowd was deafeningly loud as he stormed up
    Cheltenham hill
Winning all around and Tipperary bound for the John J
    Memorial plaque
At the speed of light it's a winner alright, the McManus Istabraq.

John Durkan's pride was deep and wide as he battled for his life
    so brave
A husband, a son full of talent and fun, a young life no-one
    could save
As each day rolls by in a place on high, he's remembered on field
    and track
While his dream rides on through a man named Swan, and a
    horse named Istabraq.

Winning every race at lightning pace to a legend in the sport of
    kings
Running every mile with grace and style, the pegasus on fleeting
    wings
He romped home free for the AIG, then the Smurfit on the
    Cheltenham track

I believe he smiled as the fans went wild for their hero Istabraq.

Another season down back to Leopardstown to win the
     Champion once again
Then across the foam he skated home where French Holly
     tried in vain
The English hope just couldn't live with the leader of the pack
It's a second feat on the Cheltenham peat for victorious Istabraq.

As his triumphs mount too many to chant, then Punchestown
     the Shell
A tour de force of the Aintree course where he added the
     Martell
His following fold, both young and old, all agree he has the
     knack
As they raise their voice for the people's choice, their beloved
     Istabraq.

It's millennium time and he's in his prime, the star of Y2K
He's Ireland's toast as he passes the post, he's a champion in
     every way
On Saint Patrick's week, he'll be at his peak when the Irish
     in Cheltenham pack
Just see him go for three in a row. Up ya boya! Istabraq.

On the night of the Champion Hurdle Davy Clifford, Pat Keating, Pat Lillis and Anita Harvey celebrated in a hotel in Cheltenham, McManus entertained his friends to dinner and Aidan O'Brien flew quietly home to Ballydoyle by helicopter. Istabraq was flown back the following day. He was scoped under sedation, but John Halley could find nothing wrong – and nothing to account for that blood on the nostril.

But O'Brien was determined to take no chances. The following Monday he issued a statement to say that it had been decided the horse should miss both Aintree and Punchestown and would not race again until the following season. For ten days after his return from Cheltenham, Istabraq's exercise was confined to walking. Only then, when there still seemed no sign of anything amiss, was he permitted to resume his normal routine, although the peace of his long hours in the stable was interrupted on several occasions by busloads of school children arriving to see the famous racehorse.

It had been planned to keep him at Ballydoyle until early May, before despatching him to Martinstown for his summer holidays – Darapour had taken over the role of companion after the death of Mister

Donovan. However, McManus became a little uneasy at the thought of Istabraq leaving all that care and attention. If something happened to the horse at Martinstown, if he got colic, for instance, he would never forgive himself. He discussed the matter with O'Brien and it was decided that Istabraq should holiday at Ballydoyle. The twenty-four hour security camera on Istabraq's box and on the whole of Margo's Yard, was extended to include the field in which he grazed.

In the current season, Istabraq's whole campaign will be geared towards his bid to become the only horse in history to win four Champion Hurdles. However, his season could well be much shorter than before and it is possible that the annual starting point of the John James McManus Memorial Hurdle will be abandoned in favour of waiting for the December Festival Hurdle at Leopardstown. This would have the advantage of avoiding a Hatton's Grace clash with Limestone Lad when the going, as well as the distance, would almost certainly be in favour of James Bowe's horse. But, with only two races before Cheltenham, it will take all Aidan O'Brien's skill to have him at his peak on the one day that matters most.

This book would not be complete without an assessment of how Istabraq compares with the previous hurdling greats and without an attempt to explain why he is so good. It is difficult to equate the Istabraq who possesses so much speed and brilliance over hurdles with the one that Willie Carson remembers as a horse who 'lacked speed and was one-paced'. Charlie Swan believes the transformation is partly due to the way the horse has been trained.

'Aidan trains everything for speed and being a good Flat trainer is all about speed,' he said. 'He has given Istabraq short bits of work over short trips and this, I am sure, has made him quicker. I really began to notice this in his second season over hurdles. Also, he likes a good pace in his races because the faster it is the better he jumps.'

O'Brien, however, is not in agreement with the Swan theory: 'I know Istabraq is trained very like a Flat horse and in his most recent season he has shown more than ever before how well he can quicken,' he said. 'But I think it is more a case of his natural ability coming through. People talk about putting speed into horses but if they haven't got it, there is no way you can put it into them.' However, Tommy Murphy has no doubt:

> What has transformed Istabraq from an ordinary Flat horse
> into a brilliant jumper are the hurdles. You have to jump well
> to be a top hurdler. It doesn't matter how good a horse is, he
> won't win a Champion Hurdle if he makes two mistakes in the
> course of the race. Istabraq's jumping is brilliant. Furthermore
> he actually likes jumping and he doesn't feel tired when he sees

another hurdle popping up in front of him. It gives him a new
lease of life.

Swan concurs with this, saying: 'Istabraq's greatest asset is undoubtedly
his jumping. He always lands running – his hind legs are down almost
before the front ones and this enables him to get away from the hurdles
so quickly. He also loves racing and he loves winning. He is a good ride,
you can settle him and he will gallop at whatever speed you want him to.
He goes on any ground and over any trip. Which way round the course
is, left-handed or right-handed, makes no difference to him. He is so
good he is almost freakish and riding him is a jockey's dream.'

So how does he compare with the greatest hurdlers of previous
years? Swan and O'Brien are the first to admit that they have not been
around long enough to offer an opinion, but Tommy Murphy has been
in racing for nearly half a century. 'Istabraq is without doubt the best
hurdler I have seen and by far,' he said. 'I saw Persian War and he was
not as good as this fellow. I also beat Comedy of Errors when I won the
Gloucester Hurdle on Noble Life in 1972. He went on to win two
Champion Hurdles, but Istabraq is a better horse.'

Hatton's Grace was the first of the triple Champion Hurdlers and
what sets him apart from the others is the age at which he recorded so
many of his big wins. He was nine when he won the Champion for the
first time in 1949 and eleven when he completed the hat-trick in 1951.
He was trained by Vincent O'Brien, not at Ballydoyle but at Churchtown
near Mallow in County Cork, and he was also a high-class performer on
the Flat. When he was ten, he won the Irish Cesarewitch under ten stone.
Istabraq would start a short-priced favourite if he were to run in the
race, but JP McManus has never shown the slightest interest in running
him on the Flat, even though Cill Dara won the 1977 Irish Cesarewitch
in his colours.

Sir Ken, trained by Willie Stephenson and ridden by Tim Molony
(who also scored on Hatton's Grace in 1951), won in 1952, 1953 and 1954,
beginning the sequence when he was five. Persian War also began his
hat-trick at the age of five in 1968 (he was trained by Colin Davies
and ridden by Jimmy Uttley), as did See You Then on whom Steve
Smith Eccles won in 1985, 1986 and 1987. See You Then suffered
from severe tendon problems almost throughout his reign and his
hat-trick represented a remarkable training achievement on the part of
Nicky Henderson.

National Hunt racing can take a terrible toll on a horse's limbs but
Istabraq has remained remarkably sound throughout his career.
However, as has been seen, his feet have frequently been a cause for
concern and so has his delicate mental make-up. He is fortunate to have

been owned by two men rich enough and understanding enough not to have put any pressure on his trainers to run him when he was not ready to do so. Indeed, he would almost certainly not have produced the performances he has if he had not been trained by such a remarkably talented man as O'Brien.

It could be argued that the only real way to compare the five triple winners is on the basis of time, and on that basis Istabraq is the best of them because he broke the course record (set by Make A Stand when he won three years earlier) by 0.3 of a second when he won for the third time. But the clock is a dangerous means of comparison. So much depends on the going and on the pace at which the race is run. Also horses, unlike athletes, are never asked to race against the clock. Furthermore, there is considerable doubt about the times at the 2000 Cheltenham meeting.

The twenty races over the three days produced eleven course records, a scarcely credible statistic that was seen by some to be the result of a firm surface, cushioned by moisture-softened earth below it. This was said to produce the ideal ground for the racehorse. Quite why it had never happened before, producing so many records at the same fixture, was not explained. Had such a succession of 'records' been recorded in Ireland, questions would have been asked about the accuracy of the clock and whether the running rail had been moved. This, though, was the Cheltenham festival and it seemed almost heresy to raise such doubts. One man who did was Dave Edwards, the timing expert of the *Racing Post Weekender*. This is what he wrote:

> On the first two days races were run on the old course and a staggering nine previous best times were shattered. When one or two winners at a meeting beat the clock, it often highlights first-rate performances but, if this many manage to do so, it usually suggests all is not as it seems. Clearly the ground was conducive to fast times – firm but well-cushioned. The fact that course records and standards over longer distances were bettered by considerably more than those over shorter trips, and by more than could be reasonably expected, strongly suggests the running rails had been moved, making the course configuration at its shortest. Athletes, swimmers and cyclists go to great lengths to improve performances by trying different clothing and equipment. Occasionally they knock hundredths of seconds off records, yet last week at Prestbury Park massive margins were knocked off. The breed may be getting better and/or faster, but not by the Alice In Wonderland amounts implied by last week's performances.

Undoubtedly the most reliable means of comparison are Timeform ratings as these are calculated by some of the most expert handicappers in racing and are based on form. They also provide consistency between one season and another. Unfortunately Timeform did not rate jumpers on an annual basis before 1962 and so it is not possible to compare Istabraq with Hatton's Grace and Sir Ken. However, these are the ratings given to the Champion Hurdlers by Timeform:

1962	Anzio	172	1982	For Auction	174
1963	Winning Fair	169	1983	Gaye Brief	175
1964	Magic Court	174	1984	Dawn Run	173
1965	Kirriemuir	166	1985	See You Then	166
1966	Salmon Spray	175	1986	See You Then	173
1967	Saucy Kit	166	1987	See You Then	173
1968	Persian War	176	1988	Celtic Shot	170
1969	Persian War	176	1989	Beech Road	172
1970	Persian War	179	1990	Kribensis	169
1971	Bula	176	1991	Morley Street	174
1972	Bula	176	1992	Royal Gait	164
1973	Comedy of Errors	178	1993	Granville Again	167
1974	Lanzarote	177	1994	Flakey Dove	166
1975	Comedy of Errors	178	1995	Alderbrook	174
1976	Night Nurse	178	1996	Collier Bay	170
1977	Night Nurse	182	1997	Make A Stand	165
1978	Monksfield	177	1998	Istabraq	172
1979	Monksfield	180	1999	Istabraq	177
1980	Sea Pigeon	175	2000	Istabraq	180
1981	Sea Pigeon	175			

Istabraq is therefore the equal of the gallant Monksfield, but 2lb below Night Nurse. Really, there is only one way that he can prove himself better than his predecessors and that is to win the Champion Hurdle for a fourth time. It will not be easy – Hatton's Grace, Sir Ken and Persian War all attempted to do just that and each was beaten, while See You Then was so badly injured in his prep race that he had to be retired. He did make a comeback and try once more, but he too was beaten in the attempt.

If, in March 2001, Istabraq succeeds where they all failed, then – and only then – will he be entitled to be regarded as the greatest hurdler of all time.

Istabraq Race Record

1994

Nov 4 DONCASTER
(soft) EBF Flanders Maiden Stakes (Div 1) (2-y-o) 7f

1	Grandinare	9-0	S. Whitworth	15-2
2	Out On A Promise	9-0	M. Hills	3-1 fav
3	Salaman	9-0	T. Quinn	8-1
4	White Heat	8-9	J. Carroll	33-1
5	Fasih	9-0	M. Roberts	8-1
6	Jalmaid	8-9	J. Fortune	50-1
7	Expansive Runner	9-0	R. Cochrane	20-1
8	Istabraq	9-0	G. Hind	8-1

sluggish start, improved stands side last two furlongs, nearest finish.

9	Advance East	9-0	M. Wigham	25-1
10	Maeterlinck	9-0	R. Street	20-1
11	Prime Property	8-9	L. Charnock	33-1
12	Bedouin Invader	9-0	K. Darley	6-1
13	Super Hero	9-0	G. Carter	9-1
14	Hong Kong Designer	8-11	J. Tate (3)	33-1
15	Nordic Breeze	9-0	W. Newnes	25-1
16	Kraton Garden	9-0	M. Tebbutt	12-1
17	Deauville Dancer	9-0	W. Woods	33-1
18	Rocky Melody	9-0	D. McKeown	33-1
19	Cashmirie	8-9	M. McAndrew	50-1

Dist: $3/4$l, $1^1/_2$l, $1^1/_4$l. Time: 1 min 34.23 sec
(M. Tabor) P. W. Chapple-Hyam

1995

April 26 KEMPTON
(good) Laburnum Maiden Stakes 1¹/₄m

1	Riyadian	3-8-8	T. Quinn	11-8 fav
2	Quandary	4-9-7	Pat Eddery	8-1
3	Kutta	3-8-8	R. Hills	16-1
4	Zidac	3-8-8	R. Perham	33-1
5	Tibetan	3-8-8	T. Ives	33-1
6	Moscow Mist	4-9-12	K. Darley	20-1
7	Polydamas	3-8-8	J. Reid	7-1
8	Braydon Forest	3-8-8	D. Harrison	50-1
9	Sea Freedom	4-9-12	J. Williams	16-1
10	Jagellon	4-9-12	M. Hills	7-1
11	Pedaltothemetal	3-7-12	A. Whelan (5)	50-1
12	Istabraq	3-8-8	W. Carson	10-1

close up till weakened over three furlongs out.

13	Pending	3-8-8	R. Cochrane	14-1
14	Pampas Breeze	3-8-3	A. McGlone	33-1
15	Dahlenburg	3-8-8	L. Dettori	10-1
16=	Sayitagain	3-8-8	W. Newnes	50-1
16=	Grandes Oreilles	3-8-3	C. Rutter	50-1
18	Elpida	3-8-8	J. McLaughlin	50-1
19	I Recall	4-9-12	S. Raymont	50-1
20	Caerle Lad	4-9-12	A. Clark	50-1
21	Great Expectations	4-9-12	M. Rimmer	50-1
22	Wizzy Lizzy	4-9-7	Paul Eddery	50-1
23	Paddy's Storm	3-8-3	J. D. Smith (5)	50-1

Dist: 3¹/₂l, 2l, sht-hd, 7l. Time: 2 min 5.74 sec
(Prince Fahd Salman) P. F. I. Cole

May 9 CHESTER
(good to firm) Christleton Maiden Stakes (3-y-o) 1¹/₄m 75yds

1	Royal Solo	9-0	B. Thomson	7-1
2	Sanmartino	9-0	M. Hills	4-1
3	Main Offender	9-0	W. Ryan	5-1
4	Mackook	9-0	W. R. Swinburn	5-2 fav
5	Berkeley Bounder	9-0	T. Quinn	20-1
6	Heath Robinson	9-0	L. Dettori	11-1
7	Hoh Express	9-0	R. Cochrane	5-1
8	Istabraq	9-0	W. Carson	11-1

*ridden along and struggling to keep in touch halfway,
some headway last two furlongs, never nearer.*

9	Baddi Quest	9-0	Paul Eddery	20-1
10	Ambidextrous	9-0	M. J. Kinane	25-1
11	Roscommon Lad	9-0	J. Reid	100-1

Dist: ³/₄l, 1¹/₄l, 5l, 2¹/₂l. Time: 2m 12.15s
(R. E. Sangster) P. W. Chapple-Hyam

July 29 NEWMARKET
(good to firm) Jif Lemon Handicap (3-y-o) 1½m

1	Silktail	8-3	G. Carter	15-8 fav
2	Istabraq	9-7	A. McGlone	4-1

with leader, led just over four furlongs out till approaching last, kept on one pace.

3	Rock Group	8-6	G. Bardwell	16-1
4	Night Time	8-11	Dane O'Neill (7)	9-2
5	Admiral's Guest	8-10	A. Clark	6-1
6	Mill Thyme	8-12	Dean McKeown	8-1
7	Lord Palmerston	9-1	K. Fallon	12-1

Dist: 1½l, nk, 13l, ½l. Time: 2 min 33.64 sec
(Mrs Monica Caine) John Berry

Aug 17 SALISBURY
(good to firm) Odstock Maiden Stakes 1¾m

1	Istabraq	3-8-5	W. Carson	5-6 on

pulled hard, tracked leaders, lost place halfway, hard ridden three furlongs out, stayed on dourly to lead inside last.

2	Dixiemelody	3-8-5	K. Darley	12-1
3	Sea Freedom	4-9-3	J. Williams	5-2
4	Arctic Charmer	3-8-5	R. Cochrane	7-2
5	Saafi	4-9-3	B. Powell	66-1
6	Salvatore Giuliano	5-9-3	T. Sprake	66-1
7	Fortunes Rose	3-8-2	D. Biggs	50-1
8	Shared	3-8-5	C. Avery	66-1
9	Andre's Affair	4-9-3	W. Newnes	66-1
10	Ceilidh Dancer	4-8-12	S. Davies	66-1

Dist: 2½, hd, 12l, 5l. Time: 3 min 7.98 sec
(Hamdan Al Maktoum) J. H. M. Gosden

Aug 30 YORK
(good to firm) Batleys Cash & Carry Handicap 1m 5f 194yds

1	Celeric	3-9-7	L. Dettori	3-1 fav
2	Istabraq	3-8-8	W. Carson	15-2

led after one furlong to two out, rallied to lead inside last, headed and no extra close home.

3	Cherrington	3-9-5	Paul Eddery	9-2
4	Floating Line	7-8-8	K. Fallon	20-1
5	Midyan Blue	5-10-0	R. Cochrane	9-1
6	Faugeron	6-8-10	Kim Tinkler	33-1
7	Star Rage	5-9-12	M. Roberts	9-1
8	Chantry Beath	4-7-11	L. Charnock	14-1
9	Cuango	4-8-11	Pat Eddery	14-1
10	Embracing	3-9-6	K. Darley	11-2
11	Augustan	4-8-0	L. Newton (5)	20-1
12	Non Vintage	4-7-8	C. Munday (7)	33-1
13	Shawahin	3-9-0	G. Carter	16-1

Dist: Hd, 1l, 1½l, 3l. Time: 2 min 59.12 sec
(Christopher Spence) D. Morley

Sep 14 AYR
(good) Rock Steady Security Handicap (3-y-o)1m 7f for the Bogside Cup

1	Istabraq	9-7	Pat Eddery	6-4 fav

made all, driven along and stayed on well final two furlongs.

2	Boundary Express	8-2	G. Hind	16-1
3	Hotspur Street	8-12	J. Weaver	25-1
4	Eau De Cologne	9-2	D. McKeown	16-1
5	Bark'N'Bite	7-10	J. Lowe	25-1
6	Court Joker	7.10	D. Gibson	20-1
7	Bowcliffe Court	8-8	D. Holland	7-1
8	Claireswan	8-6	J. Tate	13-2
9	Final Fling	7-12	J. Fanning	33-1
10	Punch	7-12	J. F. Egan	25-1
11	Noble Ballerina	7-6	D. Wright (3)	100-1
12	Greycoat Boy	8-10	M. J. Kinane	12-1
13	Island Cascade	7-7	Kim Tinkler	100-1
14	Royal York	9-4	K. Darley	14-1
15	Philmist	7-8	N. Kennedy	33-1
16	Victoria Day	7-8	L. Charnock	25-1
17	Jackmanii	7-9	T. Williams	25-1
18	Monaco Gold	7-8	K. Sked (7)	200-1
19	Swivel	9-2	K. Fallon	10-1
20	Ballard Lady	7-10	A. Mackay	40-1

Dist: 2½l, 5l, nk, ¾l. Time: 3 min 17.69 sec
(Hamdan Al Maktoum) J. H. M. Gosden

Sep 23 ASCOT
(good) Gordon Carter Handicap 2m 45yds

1	Fujiyama Crest	3-8-8	L. Dettori	8-1
2	Benfleet	4-9-9	R. Hills	20-1
3	Supreme Star	4-8-1	Dane O'Neill (5)	14-1
4	Meant To Be	5-9-0	J. Reid	20-1
5	Kristal's Paradise	3-9-2	P. Eddery	9-2
6	Lear Dancer	4-8-6	S. Sanders (3)	16-1
7	Sea Freedom	4-8-9	J. Williams	16-1
8	Pistol River	5-10-0	R. Cochrane	66-1
9	Star Player	9-8-1	J. Quinn	33-1
10	Simafar	4-8-3	B. Doyle	40-1
11	Istabraq	3-8-11	W. Carson	5-2 fav

chased leaders, ridden and lost place halfway, last and no chance five furlongs out.

12	Red Bustaan	3-8-10	M. Roberts	8-1
13	Shadirwan	4-9-0	T. Quinn	10-1
14	Witney-De-Bergerac	3-7-3	M. Dwyer (7)	40-1
15	Typhoon Eight	3-8-6	M. Hills	9-1
16	Great Crusader	3-9-5	D. Biggs	16-1

Dist: 3l, $2^1/_2$l, $^3/_4$l, 4l. Time: 3 min 33.75 sec
(Seisuke Hata) M. R. Stoute

Oct 19 NEWBURY
(good to soft) Vodafone Group Handicap 2m

1	En Vacances	3-7-12	T. Sprake	16-1
2	Istabraq	3-8-10	W. Carson	4-1

led till over four furlongs out, rallied under pressure from two out, no extra close home.

3	Purple Splash	5-9-4	W. R. Swinburn	8-1
4	Eau De Cologne	3-7-7	G. Bardwell	16-1
5	Paradise Navy	6-8-10	R. Hughes	8-1
6	Greycoat Boy	3-7-9	N. Carlisle	7-2 fav
7	Turquoise Sea	3-8-3	K. Darley	9-1
8	Bean King	9-8-13	T. Ives	20-1
9	Sweet Glow	8-8-12	M. Roberts	20-1
10	Seasonal Splendour	5-9-12	T. Quinn	9-2
11	United Front	3-8-5	D. Biggs	33-1

Dist: Nk,$1^3/_4$l, 6l, 6l. Time: 3 min 37.56 sec
(Lambourn Valley Racing) A. G. Foster

Nov 4 DONCASTER
(good to firm) Coalite Dragon Handicap 2m 110 yds

1	Merit	3-7-9	J. Quinn	2-1 fav
2	Paradise Navy	6-8-11	R. Hughes	14-1
3	Sea Victor	3-8-10	P. Robinson	12-1
4	Non Vintage	4-7-7	M. Dwyer (7)	25-1
5	Good Hand	9-9-1	M. Birch	8-1
6	Blaze Away	4-9-10	L. Dettori	11-1
7	Old Red	5-9-3	L. Charnock	15-2
8	Coleridge	7-7-8	A. Mackay	25-1
9	Inchcailloch	6-8-10	G. Bardwell	12-1
10	Istabraq	3-9-5	W. Carson	9-2

led to four furlongs out, ridden three out, faded.

11	Supreme Star	4-8-10	Dane O'Neill (5)	14-1
12	Sugar Mill	5-9-0	K. Darley	7-1
13	Thunderheart	4-8-9	G. Dutfirld	11-1

Dist: 2¹/₂l, nk, nk, 2l. Time: 3 min 39.84 sec
(Prince Fahd Salman) P. F. I. Cole

1996

June 8 HAYDOCK
(good to soft) Penny Lane Handicap 1³/₄m

1	Turgenev	7-7-13	D. Gibson	6-1
2	Istabraq	4-9-10	R. Hills	9-2

led, ridden and headed over one furlong out,
kept on same pace.

3	Riparius	5-9-8	C. Rutter	15-2
4	Anglesey Sea View	7-8-5	M. Fenton	14-1
5	Cuango	5-7-12	F. Lynch (5)	12-1
6	Satin Lover	8-8-9	S. Copp (7)	100-30 fav
7	Fabillion	4-8-11	Dean McKeown	8-1
8	Embryonic	4-9-3	J. Carroll	5-1
9	Tudor Island	7-9-7	J. Weaver	9-1
10	Highflying	10-9-10	J. Tate	12-1

Dist: 1l, 5l, ³/₄l, 1¹/₄l. Time: 3 min 7.70 sec
(Mrs Bridget Tranmer) R. Bastiman

Nov 16 PUNCHESTOWN
(soft) Locks Restaurant Novice Hurdle 2m

1	Noble Thyne	6-11-0	T.P. Treacy	4-5
2	Istabraq	4-10-9	C.F. Swan	6-4

held up, went moderate second at fourth, closed after three out, mistake next, challenged to lead approaching last, mistake and headed, ridden and rallied, stayed on near finish.

3	Saving Bond	4-10-9	R. Hughes	8-1
4	Tullabawn	4-10-9	T. J. Mitchell	25-1
5	Hollybank Buck	6-11-7	A. Powell	12-1
6	Knockaulin	5-11-0	F. J. Flood	25-1
7	Shannon Gale	4-10-9	L. P. Cusack	25-1
8	Barley Meadow	4-10-9	H. Rogers	66-1
9	Cristys Picnic	6-11-0	F. Woods	20-1
10	Cahonis	4-10-9	M. P. Hourigan	33-1

Dist: hd, 20, 11, $2\frac{1}{2}$. Time: 3 min 57.2 sec
(C. Maye) P. Mullins

Dec 1 FAIRYHOUSE
(yielding) Avonmore Royal Bond Novice Hurdle 2m

1	Istabraq	4-11-9	C. F. Swan	11-8

led early, close second, disputed fifth, led three out, clear two out, mistake last, easily.

2	Palette	4-11-4	D. J. Casey	14-1
3	Noble Thyne	6-12-0	T. P. Treacy	13-8
4	Charlie Foxtrot	4-11-9	R. Hughes	11-2
5	Three Scholars	5-12-0	R. Dunwoody	14-1
6	Lake Kariba	5-12-0	A. P. McCoy	7-1
7	Doone Braes	6-12-0	U. Smyth	200-1

Dist: $4\frac{1}{2}$, 15, 11, sh. Time: 3 min 47.8 sec
(John P. McManus) A. P. O'Brien

Dec 27 LEOPARDSTOWN
(yielding) 1st Choice Novice Hurdle 2m 2f

1	Istabraq	4-11-3	C. F. Swan	30-100

held up, went second over fifth, closed on leader approaching three out, led two out, came wide straight, clear approaching last, easily.

2	Palette	4-11-1	D. J. Casey	100-30
3	Delphi Lodge	6-11-8	Mr A. J. Martin	33-1
4	Three Scolars	5-11-8	R. Dunwoody	12-1
5	All The Vowels	5-11-4	J. P. Broderick	20-1

Dist: $5\frac{1}{2}$, 1, 14, 20. Time: 4 min 28.3 sec
(John P. McManus) A. P. O'Brien

1997

Feb 2 LEOPARDSTOWN
(good to yielding) Deloitte and Touche Novice Hurdle 2m 2 f

1	Istabraq	5-11-10	C. F. Swan	4-11

dwelt briefly, held up, 5th at 6th, went 3rd after three out, led approaching next, mistake, joined near last, slight mistake, headed briefly flat, ridden and stayed on last 100 yds.

2	Finnegan's Hollow	7-11-7	C. O'Dwyer	14-1
3	Palette	5-10-13	D. J. Casey	13-2
4	Three Scholars	6-11-7	R. Dunwoody	20-1
5	Dudley Do Right	5-11-4	N. Williamson	33-1
6	Tarthooth	6-11-13	F. Woods	13-2
7	Liss De Paor	6-11-8	T. Horgan	8-1

Dist: hd, 10, 5, 3¹/₂. Time: 4 min 22.2 sec
(John P. McManus) A. P. O'Brien

Mar 12 CHELTENHAM
(good to firm) Royal SunAlliance Novices Hurdle 2m 5f

1	Istabraq	5-11-7	C. F. Swan	6-5 fav

confidently ridden in rear, smooth headway from four out, bumped two out, driven to lead approaching last, all out.

2	Mighty Moss	6-11-7	Mr. F. Hutsby	11-1
3	Daraydan	5-11-7	R. Hughes	16-1
4	Forest Ivory	6-11-7	R. Johnson	14-1
5	Soldat	4-10-12	D. Bridgwater	33-1
6	Harbour Island	5-11-7	N. Williamson	25-1
7	Difficult Times	5-11-7	S. C. Lyons	33-1
8	Marching Marquis	6-11-7	A. P. McCoy	20-1
9	Royaltino	5-11-7	A. Kondrat	9-1
10	Hand Woven	5-11-7	C Maude	66-1
11	Boss Boyle	5-11-7	C.O'Dwyer	20-1
12	The Proms	6-11-7	C. Llewellyn	25-1
13	Nasone	6-11-7	P. Hide	100-1
14	Prussia	6-11-7	Guy Lewis	200-1
15	Hurdate	7-11-7	B. Fenton	50-1
16	Latahaab	6-11-7	L. Aspell	100-1
F	Agistment	6-11-7	R. Dunwoody	6-1

Dist: 1l, ³/₄, 3l, 7l. Time: 4 min 58.3 sec
(John P. McManus) A. P. O'Brien

Apr 23 PUNCHESTOWN
(good) Stanley Cooker Champion Novice Hurdle 2m 4f

1	Istabraq	5-11-13	C. F. Swan	4-11

close up, held up, went 2nd at 4th, mistakes four out and three out, disputed two out, soon went on, clear early straight, easily.

2	Soldat	4-11-4	R. Dunwoody	13-2
3	Boro Bow	6-11-9	T. P. Treacy	16-1
4	Ardrina	6-11-9	N. Williamson	20-1
5	Liver Bird	7-12-0	C. O'Dwyer	8-1
6	Glebe Lad	5-11-13	T. P. Rudd	20-1
7	Clonagam	8-12-0	J. Shortt	25-1
8	Liss De Paor	6-11-9	T. Horgan	10-1

Dist: 9, $^1/_2$, 10, 10. Time: 4 min 58.7 sec
(John P. McManus) A. P. O'Brien

Oct 16 TIPPERARY
(soft to heavy) John James McManus Memorial Hurdle 2m

1	Istabraq	5-11-11	C. F. Swan	6-4

held up, ran third, went second at sixth, led before straight, clear after two out, stayed on strongly.

2	Cockney Lad	8-11-11	P. Carberry	5-1
3	Bolino Star	6-11-3	T. P. Treacy	10-1
4	Colm's Rock	6-11-5	R. Dunwoody	6-1
5	Punting Pete	7-11-5	D. J. Casey	2-1
6	Native Darrig	6-11-5	Mr R. Walsh	9-2
7	Fairies Cross	7-11-5	K. Whelan	33-1
8	Rathgibbon	6-11-5	P. G. Hourigan	50-1
9	Just Little	5-11-0	N. Williamson	8-1

Dist: 7, 1, dist, $3^1/_2$. Time: 4 min 6.6 sec
(John P. McManus) A. P. O'Brien

Nov 30 FAIRYHOUSE
(yielding) Avonmore Waterford Hatton's Grace Hurdle 2m 4f

1	Istabraq	5-12-0	C. F. Swan	1-3

made all, slight mistake fourth, shaken up approaching last, ran on flat, comfortably.

2	Cockney Lad	8-12-0	P. Carberry	11-4
3	Bolino Star	6-11-4	G. Cotter	10-1
4	Gazalani	5-11-9	T. P. Treacy	20-1
5	Blushing Sand	7-11-9	Mr. T. J. Beattie	25-1

Dist: 2, 8, 13, 11. Time: 5 min 1 sec
(John P. McManus) A. P. O'Brien

Dec 29 LEOPARDSTOWN
(heavy) Agri-Business December Festival Hurdle 2m

1	Istabraq	5-12-0	C. F. Swan	1-6

*held up, fourth when slight mistake fifth, third
three out, second before two out, tracked leader,
smooth progress to dispute approaching last, led early
flat, very easily.*

2	Punting Pete	7-11-7	R. Dunwoody	14-1
3	Lady Daisy	8-11-2	A. O'Shea	11-2
4	Gazalani	5-12-0	T. P. Treacy	25-1
5	Iacchus	4-11-2	Mr. C. A. Murphy	150-1

Dist: 2¹/₂, 10, dist, 15. Time: 4 min 16.9 sec
(John P. McManus) A. P. O'Brien

1998

Jan 25 LEOPARDSTOWN
(yielding to soft) AIG Europe Champion Hurdle 2m

1	Istabraq	6-11-10	C. F. Swan	4-11

*held up in touch, fourth when mistake fifth, progress
to lead two out, narrow advantage straight, ridden
and ran on flat, went clear near finish.*

2	His Song	5-11-6	R. Hughes	8-1
3	Noble Thyne	8-11-10	G. Bradley	25-1
4	Cockney Lad	9-11-10	P. Carberry	11-2
5	Notcomplainingbut	7-11-5	T. P. Treacy	16-1
6	Theatreworld	6-11-10	N. Williamson	20-1
7	Punting Pete	8-11-10	R. Dunwoody	40-1

Dist: 1¹/₂, 3, 10, 5¹/₂. Time: 4 min 9.8 sec
(John P. McManus) A. P. O'Brien

Mar 17 CHELTENHAM
(good to soft) Smurfit Champion Hurdle Challenge Trophy 2m 110y

1	Istabraq	6-12-0	C. F. Swan	3-1 fav

always prominent, led three out, quickened clear after next, very easily.

2	Theatreworld	6-12-0	T. P. Treacy	20-1
3	I'm Supposin	6-12-0	R. Dunwoody	6-1
4	Pridwell	8-12-0	A. P. McCoy	9-1
5	Kerawi	5-12-0	C. Llewellyn	25-1
6	Mistinguett	6-11-9	C. Maude	40-1
7	Shooting Light	5-12-0	R. Farrant	66-1
8	Graphic Equaliser	6-12-0	P. Carberry	33-1
9	Relkeel	9-12-0	A. Maguire	14-1
10	Cadougold	7-12-0	M. A. Fitzgerald	25-1
11	Marello	7-11-9	P. Niven	20-1
12	Sanmartino	6-12-0	R. Johnson	20-1
13	Dato Star	7-12-0	E. Callaghan	6-1
14	Grimes	5-12-0	C. O'Dwyer	12-1
15	Lady Daisy	9-11-9	J. Titley	100-1
UR	Bellator	5-12-0	B. Fenton	100-1
PU	Red Blazer	7-12-0	J. Culloty	33-1
F	Shadow Leader	7-12-0	N. Williamson1	13-2

Dist: 12, 1, 1^1/$_4$, 4. Time: 3 min 49.1 sec
(John P. McManus) A. P. O'Brien

Apr 4 AINTREE
(heavy) Martell Aintree Hurdle 2m 4f

1	Pridwell	8-11-7	A. P. McCoy	6-1
2	Istabraq	6-11-7	C. F. Swan	4-7 fav

held up, headway sixth, challenged and hit two out, led last, hard ridden and headed near finish.

3	Kerawi	5-11-7	C. Llewellyn	10-1
4	Shooting Light	5-11-7	R. Dunwoody	12-1
5	Sanmartino	6-11-7	R. Johnson	20-1
PU	Collier Bay	8-11-7	M. A. Fitzgerald	11-2

Dist: hd, 26, 3, dist. Time: 5 min 31 sec
(Jones, Berstock and Fleet Partnership) M. C. Pipe

Nov 3 CORK
(soft to heavy) John James McManus Memorial Hurdle 2m

1	Istabraq	6-11-11	C. F. Swan	2-7

*held up, went third three out, challanged to lead
two out, soon clear, ran on well, impressive.*

2	Master Beveled	8-11-8	T. P. Treacy	10-1
3	Padre Mio	10-11-5	K. P. Gaule	33-1
4	Magical Lady	6-11-0	G. Cotter	14-1
5	Lady Daisy	9-11-0	A. O'Shea	7-1
6	Native-Darrig	7-11-5	R. Walsh	8-1

Dist: 4, 5, 3, sh. Time: 3 min 58.7 sec
(John P. McManus) A. P. O'Brien

Nov 29 FAIRYHOUSE
(yielding to soft) Avonmore Waterford Hatton's Grace Hurdle 2m 4f

1	Istabraq	6-12-0	C. F. Swan	1-5

*held up, ran moderate third, mistake fourth,
closed after four out, led next, clear before two out,
not extended.*

2	Nomadic	4-11-4	P. Carberry	11-2
3	Master Beveled	8-11-9	A. P. McCoy	8-1
4	Gazalani	6-11-9	T. P Treacy	33-1
5	Dovaly	5-11-9	T. P. Rudd	25-1
6	Blushing Sand	8-11-9	Mr. T. J. Beattie	66-1

Dist: 1/2, 6, 12, 4. Time: 5 min 4.2 sec
(John P. McManus) A. P. O'Brien

Dec 29 LEOPARDSTOWN
(heavy) Agri-Business December Festival Hurdle 2m

1	Istabraq	6-12-0	C. F. Swan	1-10

*ran moderate second, closed after three out, disputed
two out, soon led, quickened clear flat, very easily.*

2	Shantarini	4-11-2	K. P Gaule	10-1
3	Gazalani	6-12-0	T. P Treacy	20-1

Dist: 8, 15. Time: 4 min 30.4 sec
(John P. McManus) A. P. O'Brien

1999

Jan 24 LEOPARDSTOWN
(heavy) AIG Europe Champion Hurdle 2m

1	Istabraq	7-11-10	C. F. Swan	8-15

went moderate second, after first, closed after three out, challenged to lead on bridle approaching last, ran on, easily.

2	French Holly	8-11-10	A. Maguire	9-4
3	Zafarabad	5-11-6	R. Johnson	16-1
4	Theatreworld	7-11-10	T. P. Treacy	16-1
5	Nomadic	5-11-6	N. Williamson	16-1
6	Black Queen	8-11-5	A. P. McCoy	66-1

Dist: 1, 7, 2, dist. Time: 4 min 4.8 sec
(John P. McManus) A. P. O'Brien

Mar 16 CHELTENHAM
(good to soft) Smurfit Champion Hurdle Challenge Trophy 2m 110y

1	Istabraq	7-12-0	C. F. Swan	4-9 fav

tracked leaders, closed after fifth, led going well two out, pushed clear before last, ridden out run-in.

2	Theatreworld	7-12-0	T. P. Treacy	16-1
3	French Holly	8-12-0	A. Thornton	11-2
4	Mister Morose	9-12-0	C. Llewellyn	100-1
5	Nomadic	5-12-0	P. Carberry	50-1
6	Tiutchev	6-12-0	M. A. Fitzgerald	40-1
7	Bellator	6-12-0	N. Williamson	50-1
8	City Hall	5-12-0	R. Thornton	33-1
9	Lady Cricket	5-11-9	A. P. McCoy	16-1
10	Midnight Legend	8-12-0	A. Dobbin	50-1
11	Grey Shot	7-12-0	J. Osborne	33-1
12	Upgrade	5-12-0	C. Maude	66-1
BD	Blowing Wind	6-12-0	R. Dunwoody	33-1
F	Zafarabad	5-12-0	R. Johnson	40-1

Dist: $3^1/_2$, $2^1/_2$, 1, $1^1/_4$. Time: 3 min 56.8 sec
(John P. McManus) A. P .O'Brien

Apr 10 AINTREE
(good to firm) Martell Aintree Hurdle 2m 4f

1	Istabraq	7-11-7	C. F. Swan	1-2 fav

always going well and confidently ridden, smooth headway approaching three out, led on bit after last, hard held.

2	French Holly	8-11-7	A. Thornton	11-2
3	Midnight Legend	8-11-7	R. Johnson	33-1
4	Mister Morose	9-11-7	C. Llewellyn	10-1
5	Deano's Beeno	7-11-7	A. P. McCoy	10-1
F	Stretarez	6-11-7	N. Williamson	20-1
PU	Juyush	7-11-7	T. J. Murphy	25-1

Dist: 1, 6, 24, 25. Time: 4 min 43.0 sec
(John P. McManus) A. P. O'Brien

Apr 30 PUNCHESTOWN
(good) Shell Champion Hurdle 2m

1	Istabraq	7-12-0	C. F. Swan	1-4

held up, ran third, went second before two out, led early straight, ran on, easily.

2	Decoupage	7-11-9	N. Williamson	9-1
3	Limestone Lad	7-11-9	A. P. McCoy	11-1
4	Space Trucker	8-11-9	J. R. Barry	11-1
5	Sir Talbot	5-11-8	T. J. Murphy	16-1
6	Archive Footage	7-11-9	D. T. Evans	33-1
7	Feathered Leader	7-11-9	C. O'Dwyer	33-1

Dist: $3^{1}/_{2}$, 5, $5^{1}/_{2}$, $1^{1}/_{2}$. Time: 3 min 43.4 sec
(John P. McManus) A. P. O'Brien

Oct 23 TIPPERARY
(soft to heavy) John James McManus Memorial Hurdle 2m

1	Istabraq	7-11-11	C. F. Swan	2-7

Held up in touch, second before four out, joined leader between last two, led early flat, quickened clear, very easily.

2	Limestone Lad	7-11-5	P. Carberry	7-2
3	Master Beveled	9-11-8	D. Walsh	10-1
4	Samapour	5-11-5	J. R. Barry	20-1
5	Khayrawani	7-11-11	C. O'Dwyer	14-1

Dist: 7, 8, 10, $4^{1}/_{2}$. Time: 4 min 18.0 sec
(John P. McManus) A. P. O'Brien

Nov 28 FAIRYHOUSE
(soft) Duggan Brothers Hatton's Grace Hurdle 2m 4f

1	Limestone Lad	7-11-9	S. M. McGovern	13-2
2	Istabraq	7-12-0	C. F. Swan	1-7

ran moderate second, hit fifth, closed from before three out, ridden and chased winner approaching last, not reach winner flat, eased when beaten near finish.

3	Master Beveled	9-11-9	A. P. McCoy	25-1
4	Nomadic	5-11-9	P. Carberry	20-1
5	Derrymoyle	10-11-9	J. F. Titley	66-1

Dist: 5^1/$_2$, dist, 10, 6. Time: 5 min 7.0 sec
(John P. McManus) A. P. O'Brien

Dec 29 LEOPARDSTOWN
yielding to soft) A.I.B. Agri-Business December Festival Hurdle 2m

1	Istabraq	7-12-0	C. F. Swan	1-8

held up, ran third, jumped well, led two out, five lengths clear approaching last, left well clear, very easily.

2	Derrymoyle	10-12-0	P. Carberry	50-1
3	Golden Rule	4-11-2	B. J. Geraghty	10-1
4	Archive Footage	7-11-7	D. T. Evans	25-1
5	Knife Edge	4-11-6	T. P. Rudd	10-1
6	Goldanzig	4-11-2	E. G. Callaghan	50-1

Dist: 15, 9, 9, 7. Time: 4 min 5.6 sec
(John P McManus) A. P. O'Brien

2000

Jan 23 LEOPARDSTOWN
(yielding) AIG Europe Champion Hurdle 2m

1	Istabraq	8-11-10	C. F. Swan	2-9

ran second, tracked leader approaching two out, led approaching last, ran on, easily.

2	Stage Affair	6-11-10	A. P. McCoy	14-1
3	Knife Edge	5-11-6	T. P. Rudd	40-1
4	Limestone Lad	8-11-10	S. M. McGovern	9-2
5	Yeoman's Point	4-10-10	C. O'Dwyer	25-1
6	Theatreworld	8-11-10	T. P. Treacy	40-1

Dist: 4, 4^1/$_2$, nk, 12. Time: 3 min 53.9 sec
(John P. McManus) A. P. O'Brien

Mar 14 CHELTENHAM
(good) Smurfit Champion Hurdle Challenge Trophy 2m 110y

1	Istabraq	8-12-0	C. F. Swan	8-15 fav

well in touch, closed three out, tracked leader after next, led on bit last, quickened clear, impressive.

2	Hors La Loi III	5-12-0	D. Gallagher	11-1
3	Blue Royal	5-12-0	M. A. Fitzgerald	16-1
4	Ashley Park	6-12-0	T. J. Murphy	25-1
5	Stage Affair	6-12-0	A. P. McCoy	9-1
6	Dato Star	9-12-0	L. Wyer	9-1
7	Katarino	5-12-0	N. Williamson	25-1
8	Mr Percy	9-12-0	P. Hide	66-1
9	Theatreworld	8-12-0	T. P. Treacy	12-1
10	Alka International	8-12-0	A. Thornton	200-1
11	Make A Stand	9-12-0	R. Johnson	33-1
PU	Balla Sola	5-12-0	C. O'Dwyer	50-1

Dist: 4, nk, $^1/_2$, 2. Time: 3 min 48.1 sec
(John P. McManus) A. P. O'Brien

Form Comments courtesy Turf Club and *Racing Post*.

Index

Illustrations in *italic*

First published in the United Kingdom in 2000 by Cassell & Co

The picture acknowledgements below constitute an extension to this copyright page. All the pictures © photographs Pat Healy except those as follows: Peter Mooney pages 17, 21 bottom, 22 bottom, 105 top, 110 top, 111 top, 117 top; John Durkan's family pages 23, 24 top right and bottom, 42, 44, 45 top, 54 bottom; Lesley Sampson 43; John Beasley page 41 bottom; Coolmore Stud page 18 top, 19; Steven Cargill page 21 top, 22 top, 23 top; Bancroft Photography page 24 top left.

Designed by Peter Butler
Art Editor Justin Hunt

Printed and bound in England

A CIP catalogue record for this book is available from the British Library

ISBN 0 304 35628 X